# don't be
# stupid!

Lessons You Should Already Know

# Rev. R. Tony Ricard, M.Th., M.Div.

Two Knights Publishing Company
1835 St. Roch Avenue
New Orleans, Louisiana 70117

First Edition 2009

# Don't Be Stupid!

Request for permission must be addressed in writing to:
Two Knights Publishing Co.
1835 St. Roch Avenue, New Orleans, LA 70117

Printed in the United States of America

For more information about Two Knights Publishing Co. or KnightTime Ministries, please visit

www.**FatherTony**.com

All Scriptural quotations are from the New American Bible.

Book edited and cover photo by Cynthia Capen
Cover by Bjorn Jon Madrid, Graphic Designer

ISBN-13:   978-0-9793157-2-5
ISBN-10:   0-9793157-2-7

This book is dedicated
> **to the Women who have helped to form me:**
> Mrs. Iva O'Rita Honore Ricard, My Momma
> Mrs. Felicie Honore Coulon, My Nanny
>
> Mrs. Doris Westrey, my Friend and Spiritual Supporter
> Ms. Yvonne Spicuzza, Secretary, Archdiocesan Priest Personnel
> Mrs. Deidra Ricard Lopez, my Big Sister
> Mrs. Cathy Allain, my Best Friend
> Ms. Diane Dooley, my Friend and Fellow Pilgrim
> Ms. Marilyn Madine, my Business Manager
> Ms. Cynthia Capen, my Friend and Publicist
>
> **in the memory of**
>> Mrs. Anestasia Carlin Honore, my Maternal Grandmother
>> Mrs. Eva Badon Ricard, my Paternal Grandmother
>> Mrs. Grace Honore Marshall Sigur, my Momma's Big Sister
>
> **and in honor of**
>> Mary, the Blessed Mother,
>> Daughter of Anne and Joachim
>> Mother of my Lord and Savior, Jesus Christ,
>> and The Big Momma in Heaven

A Special Message to
## Rev. Mr. Melvin Jones, Deacon
Ordained to the Permanent Diaconate on December 13, 1980
Assigned to Our Lady Star of the Sea Parish, New Orleans on April 4, 2003.

Deacon, thank you for your **tireless dedication to your Diaconal Ministry**,
your **firm stance on the Battlefield of Justice**
and the **pioneering path you walked during the Civil Rights Movement**.

I pray that you will always know how much your life, your ministry and your love inspire me to be the best priest that I can be. May the words of this book and the life that I live always meet with your approval. May God bless you a hundred fold for the many ways that you have blessed me, our parish and the entire Archdiocese of New Orleans. Thank you for truly being a Deacon!

# Introduction

During my formative years, I was blessed to attend some of the most outstanding schools in the City of New Orleans and to have been taught by some of the most outstanding teachers that have ever walked the face of this Earth.

My first *school* was in the home of my Aunt Grace, my Momma's oldest sister. Aunt Grace helped to teach my cousins and me the alphabet, our basic prayers and the difference between Coca-Cola and Pepsi. I am sure that I learned how to count by watching the globe spin around on *As The World Turns!* At Our Lady of Lourdes Elementary School, my most favorite teacher was my First Grade Teacher, Mrs. Herdine Scott. Her love for her students was always evident in her ministry. (After I became a public school teacher, Mrs. Scott visited my classroom to tell me how proud she was of me. I have never forgotten that day!)

Later at St. Augustine High School, I was blessed to be inspired by Mr. Edwin Hampton (Band Director), Fr. Howard Byrd, SSJ, (Theology), and Mrs. Anne Frenier Charbonnet (Algebra). They made me proud to be a Purple Knight! When I transferred from Tulane University to Loyola University, New Orleans, Mrs. Mary Fitzgerald, professor of Elementary Education, took me under her wing and into her heart. Mrs. Fitzgerald helped to refine my gift of teaching and fueled my love for the classroom.

At Notre Dame Seminary, Fr. Stan Klores and Fr. Frank Montalbano. OMI, were very inspiring teachers. Their love for Sacred Scripture, our Church's History and their priestly ministry were always evident in their faith-filled presentations. At Xavier University's Institute for Black Catholic Studies, Fr. Joseph Brown, SJ, and Sr. Patricia Haley, SCN, were not only great teachers but, also great role models. At the Institute, they helped me to fully see the blessings of my faith, my family and my rich cultural heritage.

Indeed, I have had some of the world's best teachers. But, of all my teachers, the greatest has always been my Momma. She taught me about life and unconditional love. My love for God, my love for my family and my love for myself flows from the love of my Momma. She is a no-nonsense, "straight from the hip" mother. Rather than complicating the concept, she just "tells it like it is." I am who I am today, because she answered the Call to be a Momma.

This book is a collection of spiritual lessons that I have learned from all of my teachers, especially my Momma and my Lord and Savior, Jesus Christ. I pray that this collection of lessons will be a blessing to you and all you love.

Rev. R. Tony Ricard, M.Th., M.Div.

# Table of Contents

# SECTION ONE
## Lessons from My Momma

## Iva O'Rita Honore Ricard
### *Fr. Tony's Momma*

# Don't Be Stupid!

As I begin the reflections in this book, I need to address a rumor about me that's been going around the country. It seems that some of you have been talking behind my back and thinking that I would never find out about it. Some have been spreading this vicious rumor that could indeed be my downfall.

In fact, even some of my very own parishioners at Our Lady Star of the Sea Parish in New Orleans, Louisiana, have had the audacity, the unmitigated gall, to tell me directly the very thing that many of ya'll have apparently been saying about me for years!

You see, I have discovered that many of you have been going around this nation and telling other folks (whom I don't even know) that I am "A Momma's Boy."

"A Momma's Boy!" .... *Who me?*

Well, with this book, I want to set the record straight.
I am not a Momma's Boy.
I am not a Momma's Boy!
And, my Momma told me that I could tell you, so!
A Momma's Boy? Me? Go Figure!

But, you know, when I think about it, being called a Momma's Boy may not be so bad. First of all, if somebody messes with you, you don't have to be scared because you know that you won't have to fight alone. You know that your momma will have your back.

In fact, I have told folks in many cities throughout the United States of America and Canada that if they mess with me, "my Momma will tell my Daddy to warm up the helicopter so that she can parachute down and hurt somebody!"

So, although I am not a Momma's Boy, I am a fellow who has been lucky enough to have a Momma who knows everything, can do anything, and would whip anybody who messed with her baby. (I mean her grown-man son.)

I can give you some examples of real Momma's Boys. Bobby Boucher, from the movie, "The Waterboy," now, that's a good example of a real Momma's Boy. His Momma controlled almost everything about his life, everything about his world. And, like my Momma, she was filled with deep levels of wisdom.

For instance, when the young Bobby was talking to his Momma about girls, his Momma said, "I don't ever want you associatin' with little girls." And when he asked, "Why not, Momma?" She replied, "Because little girls are the Devil!" See, that's a Momma's wisdom!

And when he asked her, "Momma, when did Ben Franklin invent electricity?" She replied, "That's nonsense! I invented electricity. Ben Franklin is the Devil!" Once again, a Momma's wisdom!

Another infamous Momma's Boy is Forrest Gump. That boy quoted his Momma all of the time (not that quoting your Momma is a bad thing). In the movie, "Forrest Gump," Forrest said, "Momma always had a way of explaining things so I could understand them."

It's clear that is why almost all of his wisdom-filled quotes started with the phrase "Momma always says."

For example, Forrest once said, "Momma always says there's an awful lot you could tell about a person by their shoes. Where they're going. Where they've been. I've worn lots of shoes."

And, of course we all remember his popular phrase, "My Momma always said, 'Life was like a box of chocolates. You never know what you're gonna get."

One of my most favorite Forrest Gump quotes came right after his soon to be girlfriend, Jenny, asked him, "Are you stupid or something?" Forrest replied by saying, "Momma says stupid is as stupid does."

Both Bobby Boucher and Forrest Gump lived good and productive lives. Both developed into wonderful adults by listening to the wisdom of their Momma's. In looking at the successful lives of Bobby and Forrest, we can all conclude that being a Momma's Boy really isn't that bad. One can truly do well if they heed their Momma's warnings and live by their wisdom.

Bobby and Forrest both proved that being a Momma's Boy can indeed lead to great success (even though I'm not one).

Now, I do have to admit that I have been pretty successful, traveling around the country and living a life that is eerily similar to the lives of Mr. Boucher and Mr. Gump. For, just like Bobby and Forrest, I've been quoting my Momma in front of thousands and thousands of folks.

Although I am not a Momma's Boy, I do talk about my Momma during my presentations in almost every city I visit. But, of course, if you had a Momma like mine, you would, too. I think that I have been living pretty well off of the money that I've made quoting from her. (But, please don't tell her because she will want a share in the funds!)

Like Most Momma's, Iva O'Rita Honore Ricard takes her job of being a Mother and a Grandmother seriously. In fact, being a Momma is not just what she does, it is who she truly is. It is her vocation from God.

Now, my Momma has all of those usual quotes that most Momma's use. For example, if you're crying because she had just finished fussing at you or giving you a spanking, she'd say, "You better hush up or I'll give you something to cry about." (While in your mind you are thinking, "I believe that you just did!")

Or when you were misbehaving in a store, she'd say, "Oh, you can act a fool, now, but, just wait till we get home!" (Little did she know how much money I would one day make *"acting a fool"* in front of thousands and thousands of folks.) Indeed, my Momma has quite a few quotes that teach major lessons in just a few words.

The one quote from my Momma that I have used most when traveling around the United States and Canada is the one that she used to say to us when we were small as we were leaving the house. She would always look at us and say,
**"Remember who you belong to and Don't Be Stupid."**

Now, the "Remember who you belong to" part was simple to understand. As her children, we knew we represented her wherever we would go. In school, in Church and in the neighborhood, folks knew that she was our Momma and that we were her kids. Therefore, whatever we did (be it good or bad) was a reflection on her parenting skills. So, we had better make sure that we "represented her well." Because if we didn't "act right," it was going to be "ugly" when we got home!

Now, the 'Don't be Stupid" part is what used to confuse my friends. They would always ask if our Momma was calling us, "Stupid." But, we would explain that she was telling us "not to be stupid." She not was saying, "You *are* stupid."

One of the very first lesson that we learned early in life was that *ignorance is when you don't know something.* If you don't know that it is wrong, you can plead ignorance. But, *stupidity is when you know something is wrong but you still do it!* You can't plead ignorance, you are just stupid!

4

Therefore, if you really want to be a success in life, all that you need to do is "Remember who you belong to and Don't Be Stupid."

In a Momma Boucher and a Momma Gump kind of way, those few words from my Momma basically summed up everything we needed to know about life, about faith and about our relationship not only with our family but also with our God.

If we live our lives remembering who we belong to and trying hard not to be stupid, I believe that we can indeed be successful here on Earth and one day find ourselves celebrating in the Kingdom of Heaven. Because, in a very real way.

I believe that the entire Bible and almost everything our Church has taught over the span of the last 2000 plus years can be summed up in the simple phrase, "Remember who you belong to and Don't Be Stupid."

## Remember who you belong to!

First, we all ought to remember that we ultimately belong to God. From the moment he knit us in our Mother's wombs, He claimed us as His own.

In the Book of the Prophet Isaiah, it reads,

> *"Thus says the LORD, who created you, O Jacob,*
> *and formed you, O Israel: Fear not, for I have redeemed you;*
> *I have called you by name: you are Mine.*
>
> *When you pass through the water,*
> *I will be with you; in the rivers you shall not drown.*
>
> *When you walk through fire, you shall not be burned;*
> *the flames shall not consume you.*
>
> *For I am the LORD, your God,*
> *the Holy One of Israel, your Savior."*[1]

As the Sons and Daughters of God , we are Co-heirs to the Kingdom!
Thus, when we leave this world and are born into Heaven, we will be returning back home to our Daddy's House. We belong to Him!

---

[1] Isaiah 43:1-3

St. Paul in his Second Letter to St. Timothy reminds all Christians to *"Bear your share of hardship for the Gospel with the strength that comes from God."*[2] In other words, regardless of what you may be going through, "Remember who you belong to."

Remember that even when it gets tough, you belong to God and must represent Him in good times and in bad times. *You are a Child of God.* So, act like one and remember to represent our Heavenly Daddy to the best of your ability!

You must always remember that God is not looking for a part-time lover. You have to be a full-time Christian, even when it gets tough. You had better remember that it was God and not this world, that saved us! Thus, wherever we go, we ought to remember who we belong to!

Now, the "Don't Be Stupid" part, believe it or not, that's in the Bible and our Church's teachings, too.

You see, God, the Church and my Momma taught me that we should *Do unto others as we would have them do unto us.*[3] I was taught to live by the Laws of God and the Ten Commandments. I was also taught to "always be nice" and to try to be grateful for whatever God and others give me. I am sure that most of the Mommas in the world have also tried to teach the same things to their children.

That is why I always tell teens that by the 9th Grade, you already know everything you need to know about life. You already now "right from wrong." You know that illegal drugs are bad. You know that pre-marital sex is wrong and that both the physical and emotional consequences of such acts can destroy your life. You should also know about the dangers of drunk driving.

So, if you go out and engage in any of these life altering and possibly life ending acts, you can't say you didn't know. You can only say that you were stupid!

How much better our lives would be if the official Church Theologians would just sum up all that God has been trying to teach us by saying, "Remember who you belong to and Don't Be Stupid."

Maybe then, folks wouldn't be living lives that definitely don't reflect the Love of God or their desire to be with Him one day in Heaven.

---

[2] 2 Timothy 1:8

[3] Matthew 7:12

6

Maybe then, teens wouldn't get so confused by our theological language and would better understand the core of what we believe and why we believe it.

Maybe then, folks would begin to realize that ignorant folks might make it into Heaven, but the stupid will only perish in Hell.

If *ignorance is when you don't know something* and *stupidity is when you know something is wrong but you still do it,* then we can be sure that the stupid person who does not repent and turn back to God will indeed end up in Hell with a whole bunch of other stupid people.

After reflecting on my Momma's wisdom, I guess that I have to admit that at some level, I really am a Momma's Boy.

In fact, I have told folks that when I die, all that they need to put on my grave headstone is simply this, "He Loved the Lord and the Lord loved Him, and of course, he was his Momma's Baby!"

Today, I hope that you have learned a little bit from this Momma's Boy and from the wisdom of His Momma.

Today, I say to you, in the name of Jesus and your Momma,
"Remember who you belong to and Don't Be Stupid."

"Remember you are God's Child and Don't Be Stupid."

Wherever you go, represent our God in the ways that He has called us to represent Him. And, if you are tempted to fall into the traps of the Devil, *"Don't Be Stupid."*

And if by chance, you are doing something that you know is wrong, "STOP. That's all. Just stop!"

Because, "stupid is as stupid does." And, you don't need to be stupid anymore.

May God give us the strength to live a life worthy of His Name.
May He bless us with His protection and grace.
And, may He give us the strength to not be stupid any more.

People of God, using the words of my Momma, I say to you,

**"Remember who you belong to and Don't Be Stupid."**

# Shut Up and Just Listen!

A Message to My Teenage Brothers and Sisters.....and to the Grown Folks, too!

Alex Trebek the host of the TV game show, *Jeopardy,* once said, "It's very important in life to know when to shut up!"

But, unfortunately, most people don't know when that point is!

In relationships, like with a girlfriend or boyfriend,
> sometimes you ought to *Shut Up and Just Listen!*

In relationships with your parents,
> sometimes you ought to *Shut Up and Just Listen!*

In relationships with yourself,
> sometimes you ought to *Shut Up and Just Listen!*

And most definitely in your relationship with God,
> sometimes you ought to *Shut Up and Just Listen!*

I assure you that at age 13, 14, 15 or even 18 years old, you do not know everything that there is to know about life! You really don't know everything. So, sometimes you need to *Shut Up and Just Listen* to what others have to say.

*Shut Up right now and Just Listen!*

Turn off the music.

Turn off the television.

Turn off the computer.

And close your mouth!

Right now, all you need to do is Shut Up right now and Just Listen! ('Cuz you just might learn something.)

Not only do you need to Shut Up. If there is someone in your life that is talking so much that they are causing you to miss whatever it is that God is trying to tell you, tell them to Shut Up, too.

8

My young brothers and sisters,

God indeed has a lot that He wants to say to us. But, first we have to be ready to listen. First, we have to be willing to tune our ears to the voice of God. We have to be ready to listen because God has some really cool things that He wants us to know.

From the very beginning of time, God has been trying to tell us stuff.

First of all, He wants to tell us how much He loves us and that He is willing to do anything that He can to make sure that we feel His love.

In the Book of Genesis, for example, God, himself, talked directly to us. Time and time again, God spoke directly to Adam and Eve. He told them how much He loved us by first, giving them dominion over the whole world. That means that everything on Earth was created for us to enjoy. *That's* how much God loves us. Everything that the eye can see was made for us. To God, we are the peak of Creation. We are His children.

God also loves us enough to give us a perfect gift: The gift of a free will. He loves us so much that He gave us the complete freedom to choose to do right or wrong.

We can freely choose to love God with our whole hearts, our whole minds and our whole souls. And, we can freely choose to love our neighbors as we love ourselves.

Talk about a message of True Love from God!

In the Hebrew Scriptures[4], God also talks to those He loves through His blessed messengers, the "visitors" or angels.

Angels bring us messages from the Lord. The visitors that stopped by to see Abraham were angels. The visitors that tended to the care of Isaiah, were angels, too. And, of course, the figures that Jacob saw ascending and descending on a ladder that reached up to Heaven, were messengers or angels from the Lord. From the very beginning of time, the Lord has been speaking to us and sending us Messages of Love.

---

[4]The Hebrew Scriptures is another name for The Old Testament.

9

Even when we are stupid and are choosing to do stuff that we know that *God did not want us to do*, God is still sending us Messages of Love.

The Ten Commandments[5] are perfect examples of Loving Messages that the Lord wanted to send us. Although some have seen the Ten Commandments as rule on what we should not do, they really are Messages from God that remind us just who we are to God and how He wants us to show His Love to the world.

The first parts of the Ten Commandments remind us that we should Love God above everything. The rest of the Commandments tell us that we should love everyone else and treat them right. But, we all know that even after we got the Commandments, we still wanted to do stuff our way. We didn't want to shut up and listen to God.

Humans have got to be the most *hard-head'est* creatures on the face of the Earth.[6] As free as we are, we still can't figure out how much God loves us and how we are supposed to respond to that love. Some even want to tell God how He is supposed to be God.

I think that there have been many times in our history that God has wanted to yell down from Heaven, "Shut Up and Just Listen to Me!"

But, nooooo, we don't want to do that.

Oh nooooo, Heaven forbid we Shut Up and Listen to the Lord!

But, that is exactly what God wants us to do.

He especially needs the young folks in our world to Shut Up and Just Listen. Because, we already have too many grown folks who are so set in their ways that they will never ever get to experience what God has in store for those who love Him. There are way too many grown folks who I believe think that they are God.

I can't wait to get to Heaven to see their faces when they get to the Judgment Seat and find out that not only are they not God, but, because they thought that they were, they will get to see where the Devil lives.

---

[5]See Deuteronomy 5:1-21 and Exodus 20:1-17

[6]I don't know if *"hard-head'est"* is actually a word. If it isn't, it is now! So, the dictionary should give me credit for creating it.

(Remember, Satan didn't want to listen to God because he thought that he was equal to God, too.)

That's why God needs you to pay attention to what He has to say.

You young people must realize, God really does need you!

In the Old Testament, God spoke to a good deal of young folks. And, was able to use them to bring His Word to the world. Through many young folks, God was made present to those He loves.

Shadrach, Meshach and Abednego are good examples of young guys that God used to send a message to the world. They were the three guys whom Nebuchadnezzar was trying to burn in a fire because they did not want to blaspheme against God, worship a false God and reject His love.

When they were put into the fire, the three of them began to pray to the Lord and testify to His goodness. As they prayed, the fire never harmed them. In fact, those who witnessed their defiant acts of love and prayer, saw what looked like an angel walking in the fires with them. As a result of their faith, their oppressors were changed and began to join the guys in praising the God of Abraham!

For those boys, praying in that fire was their way of telling their torturers, Shut Up and Just Listen!

Another young person that God used to bring His Messages to the world was the Prophet Jeremiah. Jeremiah was one of the youngest prophets ever called by the Lord to His service. Jeremiah was also very reluctant to listening to God and accepting His call to ministry.

When God called Jeremiah, this soon-to-be prophet tried to get out of it by using one of the lamest excuses that I have ever heard.

In Jeremiah 4:1-10, God speaks directly to Jeremiah, saying,

> *Before I formed you in the womb I knew you,*
> *before you were born I dedicated you,*
> *a prophet to the nations I appointed you.*

> *"Ah, Lord GOD!" I said,*
> *"I know not how to speak; I am too young."*

*But the LORD answered me, Say not, "I am too young."*
*To whomever I send you, you shall go;*
*whatever I command you, you shall speak.*

*Have no fear before them,*
*because I am with you to deliver you, says the LORD.*

*Then the LORD extended his hand and touched my mouth,*
*saying,*
*See, I place my words in your mouth!*

*This day I set you over nations and over kingdoms,*
*To root up and to tear down, to destroy and to demolish,*
*to build and to plant.*

*The word of the LORD came to me with the question:*
*What do you see, Jeremiah?*[7]

When God called Jeremiah to service, Jeremiah tried to get out of it by saying he was "too young" for God to use him. But, the Lord cut him off by yelling to him, *"Say not I am too young."*

Jeremiah was trying to tell God that he was not ready to do what the Lord needed him to do. But, the Lord told him that he was not going to accept that lame excuse of "I am too young." God need Jeremiah to be his prophet, to be his messenger. That is why I believe that when God say to Jerry, "Say not I am too young," God was basically saying to Jeremiah, "Shut Up and Just Listen!"

God, has always needed young folks like the three boys in the fire and Jeremiah to be His messengers to the world. He has always wanted to see the younger generation step up to the tasks of being *real* Disciples of God. The Lord loves us so much that He gave us this world and has prepared an even better world for us when we get to Heaven.

In the Gospels, we discover that God found an even better way to talk to us and to send us His Messages of Love. And, He used a young teenaged girl to make that way of talking to us possible.

_____

[7]Jeremiah 1:4-11a

When the Lord sent the Angel Gabriel to Mary to talk about love and to ask her to be the *one who would bear the purest form* of *love* into the world, God told Mary, "Girl, I need you to help me to do what I need to do for my children."

But, at first, Mary wasn't really ready to hear what God had to say. That is why her first response to God was, *"How can this be, since I have no relations with a man?"*[8]

To help her understand, Gabriel had to explain to Mary that the Holy Spirit was going make it happen. Because, with God, all things are possible.[9] When Gabriel said to Mary, "All things are possible," he was essentially saying to her, "Shut Up and Just Listen!"

Well, we all know the *rest of the story*.

Mary did indeed shut up. And through this young girl, God brought pure joy into the world. Through this teenaged girl, God brought Salvation to those *who were lost*. Through this young teenaged girl, God brought His only Begotten Son into the world to show us the way to the Kingdom of Heaven. All because, Mary, a young teenage girl, was willing to Shut Up and Just Listen!

As we look into the life of Mary's Baby Boy, Jesus, we can see that God wanted to talk to us so badly that He came down to Earth to do it directly. Since folks had stopped listening to Him through the ministry of the prophets, God knew that He needed to come down *HIMSELF* and bring His messages to us.

In Jesus, we have been given the greatest opportunity to hear what God has to say to us. Because, Jesus is indeed *God-Incarnate*.

In Jesus, God says to us, I love you so much that I am willing to do whatever I have to do to help you make it home to me in Heaven. God the Father wanted the whole world to know just who Mary's Baby Boy is.

That is why at the Baptism of the Lord, Our Heavenly Father opened the Heavens, sent the Holy Spirit down in the form of a Dove and said to the world, *"This is My Beloved Son; with You, I am well pleased."*[10]

---

[8]Luke 1:34

[9]Luke 1:37 says, *"Nothing will be impossible for God."*

[10]Luke 3:22

In a very real way, God was telling us and the whole world, that Jesus was His Baby Boy and is His greatest communication to the world. When you think about it, we are extremely blessed to be living in the time and era that we are now living. The life we have now is so much better than the life of the prophets of the Old Testament.

First, we don't have to eat some of the stuff they ate, like locusts and wild honey.[11] Since I am a picky eater, and I don't like to eat green stuff like vegetables, I know that I would hate eating locusts and wild honey!

But, more importantly, we have something that they longed to have. We have something that they dreamed about. We have the presence of Jesus, the Messiah, in our lives.

As tough as it may be to understand, having Jesus in our lives makes our earthy lives far better than even the life that Moses lived! Although it might have been nice to be one of the Prophets from the Old Testament, I would never chose to trade places with them. There is no way that I would want to live a life in which I would still be longing for a Savior.

After Jesus grew up and was ministering in His land with the help of His boys, the Apostles, God the Father still wondered if folks were getting His Message of Love. He wondered if folks were listening to Him.

So, God the Father led Jesus, Peter, James and John up the mountain to talk a little bit about what He wanted us to do. In the blessed events of the Transfiguration of our Lord, Jesus was transfigured and transformed right before the eyes of His three boys.

And, as they gazed upon the Glorified and Radiant Lord, as He stood in the presence of the Prophets Moses and Elijah, they heard the voice of our Heavenly Father say to them and to us, *"This is My Beloved Son, Listen to Him."* [12]

In saying, *"This is My Beloved Son, Listen to Him,"* God the Father was basically saying to the Apostles and to us, *"Shut Up and Just Listen. Jesus Has Something to Say!"*

That is why we have to stop and pay attention to what Jesus has to tell us.

---

[11]Matthew 3:4

[12]Mark 9:2-13

He has, as Peter would put it, *"the words of eternal life."*[13]

Jesus' Words to us not only speak about life, they also can bring us back to life.

His words are words of healing.
His words are words of peace.
His words are words of love.

But, we can't get that healing, peace or love for our lives if we are not willing to *Shut Up and Just Listen* to Him!

Today, Jesus once again says to us, *"Ephphatha."*
He says to us, *"Talitha koum."*
He says to us, *"Eli, Eli, lema sabachthani?"*

*"Ephphatha"* means *"be opened."*
*"Talitha koum"* means *"Little girl, I say to you, arise!"*
*"Eli, Eli, lema sabachthani?"* which means, *"My God, my God, why have you forsaken me?"*

In His Words, we can find all that we need to know about His love for us and the love that we should have for Him.

When He touched the ears and mouth of a deaf and mute man, Jesus said to him, *"Ephphatha."*[14] With that simple touch and that simple word, the deaf man was healed was able to hear clearly the messages that Jesus came to bring.

When He walked into the room where Jairus' Daughter had died, He gently touched her and said, *"Talitha koum."*[15] And, the dead girl came back to life.

As He hung upon the tree, dying for our sins through no fault of His own, He screamed out, *"Eli, Eli, lema sabachthani?"*[16] In these words, Jesus was *telling us* and *showing us* how much He loved us. Through His words, we can see that Jesus was willing to die, even though He was afraid.

---

[13]John 6:68

[14]Mark 7:34

[15]Mark 5:41

[16]Matthew 27:46

My young brothers and sisters,

If only we could be like Peter, James and John...
If only we would be like that deaf man or that dead girl...
If only we would just Shut up and Listen!

Can you even imagine what it would be like to see Jesus transfigured and transformed?

That's why we have to learn *how to be deaf* to some of the things in this world. We have to be deaf to some of the bad things that are influencing our lives, our thought patterns and our choices.

We have to turn off some of the music that is influencing us. We have to turn off some of the websites that are influencing us. We have to turn off the TV and even the voices of some of our *so-called* friends, if we truly want to be deaf enough to hear what Jesus as to say. We have to be deaf to this world in order to have Jesus come to us and say, *Ephphatha* - be opened! *We have to Shut Up and Just Listen to Him!*

We also have to choose to die to the things of this world, if we truly want to be His disciples. Like Jairus' Daughter, Jesus wants to touch us and say, *"Talitha koum"* means "Little girl, I say to you, arise!" But first, we really have to die: not die in a physical sense, but die in a spiritual sense to the ways of this world so that we can be *Born Again* in the Spirit.

We also have to be willing to stand at the foot of the cross and listen to the Lord as He cries out to His Father. We have to stand right next to Mary and the Beloved Disciple, as the Lord looks up to Heaven and cries out, *"Eli, Eli, lema sabachthani?"*

We have to be there because as He cries out, He is crying not only for Himself, but He cries out for us, too. First, He is praying that we, too, will not abandon Him. And second, He is asking the Father to never abandon us.

As he hung on that cross, Jesus was saying to all of us,

*"Please, Please Shut Up! Please just listen to what I am saying to you! I love you! I love you! I love you so much that I am willing to take this pain so that you might have life and have it more abundantly.*

*I love you......So, Please Just Shut Up and Listen to Me!"*

The greatest Message of Love that Jesus gave us was right there on Calvary.

By hanging on the cross, He was telling us *why* God made us and who we are called to be. In the Crucifixion, Jesus allowed His actions to say all that He needed to say. In the Crucifixion, we can truly see that *Actions Speak Louder than Words!*

Now, it is up to us to respond to His words and actions of love. Now, it is up to us to do what we have to do to return to Him the love that He has given to us. Now, we have to Shut Up and Just Listen as Jesus says to us,
*"Ephphatha."*
*"Talitha koum."*
*"Eli, Eli, lema sabachthani?"*

Now is the time for us to be still and know that God is still God.

Now is the time for us to be like the waves and the seas, and hear Jesus say to us, *"Quiet! Be still!"*[17]

Now is the time for us to have folks look at us just as the Disciples looked at the calm waters of that once storm driven sea and say, *"Who then is this whom even wind and sea obey?"*[18] They need to be looking at us and saying, *"Who then is this whom even* this Knuckle Head and that Knuckle Head obey?"

Today, we are all challenged by God to be like Shadrach, Meshach and Abednego. We are challenged to be like Isaiah and Jeremiah; to be like Peter, James and John and simply, *Shut up and Just Listen!*

In Jesus Christ, God, the Father, says to us,
　　　*"This is My Beloved Son, Listen to Him."*

Young People, in the Name of Jesus I say to you,
　　　*"Shut Up and Just Listen. Jesus Has Something to Say!"*

---

[17]Mark 4:39

[18]Mark 4:41

# Don't Worry:
# Your Daddy Knows the Way

When I was a child, my family used to take little vacation trips to various places throughout the South. For one or two weeks during the summer, we would all pile up into my Dad's old Bonnabel Station Wagon, and head in some unknown direction.

Though my brother, my sister and I rarely knew where we were going, my Dad always had a fun destination in mind.

One summer, he took us on a trip along the Gulf Coast. We must have visited every little towns along the Mississippi Coast. We played on the beach, swam in the Gulf of Mexico and ate at many of the little restaurants along the way.

During another summer, my Dad decided to take us to Astroworld in Houston, Texas. However, my Mom wanted to go to Vicksburg, Mississippi, her birthplace. Now, geographically, Houston is to the west of New Orleans and Vicksburg is to the north. But, my Dad devised a plan to take us to Houston by way of Vicksburg.

Although it was a very very long ride in the car, we had fun in both locations.

Back in the old days, my family thoroughly enjoyed going on our summer trips. We have always loved being together. Our little trips gave us a lot of quality time together and that was great.

I can remember one family trip when we were headed back home driving down on old country road near New Roads, Louisiana when one of those heavy summer-time thunderstorms hit. Rain clouds hovered the road and soon drenched the highway with tons and tons of water.

The rain was so heavy that you could barely see 10 feet in front of the car. I can remember being terrified, and asking my Momma if we were going too fast.

Though my Mother was probably scared herself, she turned to me and said gently, *"Don't worry. Your Daddy knows the way."*

You see, my Dad spent many summers walking along that old country road. It was the same road along which most of his family once lived.

He had walked that road when there was no money to buy gasoline. He rode his bike on that blacktop to go visit his family. And for years, he had made those yearly trips back down that road to see his people.

Yes, Dad indeed knew where we were going (I already knew that). But, it sure did help to hear my Momma say, *"Don't worry. Your Daddy knows the way."*

Indeed, comfort comes when we realize that the drivers in our lives know where we are going. Quite a long time ago, our Heavenly Father made a promise to our Premiere Patriarch, Abraham. God told him that He would always be our Father and that we would be His people. He would always be the Driver in our collective Station Wagon of Life.

When we were lost, afraid or unable to find our way, He would be there to guide us and to bring us home.

If necessary, He would bear us up on Eagles Wings to bring us home to Himself .[19] As long as we kept His Commandments, we would be marked as His chosen family.

But, we know that there have been times in our lives when we have either forgotten or taken for granted the fact that we have been chosen to be God's very special children. There are times in our lives when we fail to remember that He is our Father in Heaven. It is in these times that we fall into the traps of sin: somehow losing sight of the path on which we have been called to travel.

Sin becomes like summertime thunder storms on old country roads: using blinding rains to block our vision of our true destination: our true purpose.

But, in the *Letter to the Romans*, St. Paul reassures us that God will not leave us alone in the thunderstorms of sin to find our own way back to Him. In fact, God has promised to take control of the wheel and guide us safely home.[20]

In the person of Jesus Christ, God, our Creator, has provided a driver for our Heavenly Bound Station Wagon. Through His death and resurrection, we have been given a clear path through the heavy rains of sin and the strong winds of temptation. Though we are sinners, God still calls each of us by name and invites us to the homecoming banquet of the reconciled.

---

[19]See Exodus 19:2-6

[20]See Romans 5:6-11

Just as a Father and a Mother are called to love each of their children, unconditionally, God loves each and every member of this one united family in Christ. God is willing to do whatever it takes to protect each and every member of His Chosen People. He will give all that He has for the sake of just one of us.

In fact, that is just what God did for us. Our Heavenly Father proved His love for us by giving us the greatest gift possible: Jesus Christ, *God His-very-self.*

For, what more could He possibly give?

Nothing could surpass the gift of His only begotten Son.

We come to know God's love through the actions of Jesus Christ, through the ministry of the Apostles, through the love shares with us by our individual families and through the Grace of our church family.

In a very real way, we can sense God's loving presence because God has stopped at nothing to bring us into His Sheepfold. Just like the apostles, God, our Father, has called each of us by name. He has given us very special gifts: gifts which are to be used for the sake of our families.

Each of us is called to be a minister of God's love in the way and in the place God has called us.

Some are called to be spouses; to be Husbands or Wives.
Some are called to be parents; to be Fathers or Mothers.
Some are called to be ordained; to be Priests or Deacons.
Some are called to enter Religious Life; to be Religious Sisters and Brothers.

Whatever your role in life is, you must realize that God has given you a simple command, *"Without cost you have received; without cost you are to give."*[21] or simply, *The gift you have received, give as a gift.* We know that when we share the gifts God has given us, those gifts are multiplied within us and new gifts are formed.

Sometimes, traveling down the country roads of life can be difficult. When storms arrive, many people choose to stop on the side of the road hoping that the storms will somehow pass them by.

---

[21]Matthew 10:8

But, my brothers and sisters, those who are truly committed to the love of God and have come to accept Jesus Christ as the Driver of their Station Wagons, do not have to stop and wait for a guide. For, we know that God, Our Heavenly Father, has traveled this way a million times before.

He traveled through the thunder storms of sin and disappointment when He guided the feet of Moses and the Israelites. He traveled through the strong winds of temptation when He sent Jesus to die on our behalf. He traveled through the blistering winds and the blinding rains of human frailty when He called the Twelve Apostles to cure the sick, raise the dead, heal the leprous and expel demons.

Yes, God, Our Father, has indeed traveled down these roads before and He knows our ultimate destination: the greatest vacation spot . . . a seat at the family table in Heaven.

How blessed are we to have God as the Driver in our Station Wagons.

Yes, God, the Father,  does indeed know where we are going.

We already know that . . .
> He sent Jesus to show us the way.

For Jesus says, *"I am the way and the truth and the life."*[22]

But, when we are in the midst of the storms, it sure does help to hear my Momma say, *"Don't worry. Your Daddy knows the way."*

# Mr. Rodney J. Ricard
## *Fr. Tony's Daddy*
### August 1955

---

[22]John 14:6

# Let God Be the Judge!

As a proud grandmother, my mother has taken on many chores to help my brother and my sister care for their own children. Between my brother's son and two daughters and my sister's two sons, I assure you that my Momma's hands are definitely full with her many grandmotherly duties. And, when you also throw in the young guys that I mentor, she really has a lot to handle as the matriarch of our clan.

Back when my nephews were still in elementary school, much of her grandmotherly chores revolved around playing chauffeur to her young bundles of joy. Each day, she had the task of driving them to and from school or summer camp. And , she provided free after-school and after-camp-care services.

A few years ago, my mom along with three of her grandkids were arriving at my parents' home, after she had picked them up from summer camp, when she noticed that the neighbor had graciously cut the grass in the front of her house. Apparently, while he was out cutting the grass in his own front yard, he saw that my parents' grass could use some attention.

Now, if you've seen a New Orleans lawn following our usual stretch of summertime thunderstorms, you would know that the lawn definitely needed attention. So, he cut it for them. Needless to say, she was quite thankful that her neighbor performed this great act of charity. The lawn looked nice and made that her feel good. But, when she looked over at her prized cement planter, her elation soon ended.

You see, the neighbor's children decided to also help her out. But, instead of helping with the grass, they attempted be helpful by pulling the weeds from her little garden. The only problem was *the children had no idea which green stems with leaves were weeds and which were my Momma's actual plants.*

Therefore, these six and seven year olds worked hard to pull out of the garden anything they thought were weeds. Out went the Gladiolus, out went the Ivy, and out went most of the plants that my mom had been nurturing for years inside that planter. The only plants that survived the weeding were the plants that had the deepest deep roots.

Obviously, the words she used when she saw her planter were not words of gratitude that could be repeated on the Altar of the Lord or in a book that was written by her son, The Priest!

Although they thought that they were helping her, the neighbor's kids really did a number on her little garden.

When I was reading the Parable of the Wheat and the Weeds from the Gospel according to our Brother Matthew, I though about my Momma's little garden. In this parable, Jesus tells us that one day, God will be like those kids who helped my Momma weed her garden. On the Final Judgment Day, God will return to gather up His Faithful Followers and bring them to Heaven. Those who are not faithful to His Word will find themselves being thrown into the fiery furnace.

> *"The Kingdom of Heaven may be likened to a man who sowed good seed in his field. While everyone was asleep his enemy came and sowed weeds all through the wheat, and then went off.*

> *When the crop grew and bore fruit, the weeds appeared as well. The slaves of the householder came to him and said, 'Master, did you not sow good seed in your field? Where have the weeds come from?'*

> *He answered, 'An enemy has done this.' His slaves said to him, 'Do you want us to go and pull them up?'*

> *He replied, 'No, if you pull up the weeds you might uproot the wheat along with them. Let them grow together until harvest; then at harvest time I will say to the harvesters, 'First collect the weeds and tie them in bundles for burning; but gather the wheat into my barn.'"*

> *He proposed another parable to them. "The Kingdom of Heaven is like a mustard seed that a person took and sowed in a field. It is the smallest of all the seeds, yet when full-grown it is the largest of plants. It becomes a large bush, and the 'birds of the sky come and dwell in its branches."*

> *He spoke to them another parable. "The Kingdom of Heaven is like yeast that a woman took and mixed with three measures of wheat flour until the whole batch was leavened."*

> *All these things Jesus spoke to the crowds in parables. He spoke to them only in parables, to fulfill what had been said through the prophet: "I will open my mouth in parables, I will announce what has lain hidden from the foundation (of the world)."*

*Then, dismissing the crowds, He went into the house. His disciples approached Him and said, "Explain to us the parable of the weeds in the field."*

*He said in reply, "He who sows good seed is the Son of Man, the field is the world, the good seed the children of the Kingdom. The weeds are the children of the evil one, and the enemy who sows them is the Devil. The harvest is the end of the age, and the harvesters are angels. Just as weeds are collected and burned (up) with fire, so will it be at the end of the age. The Son of Man will send His Angels, and they will collect out of His Kingdom all who cause others to sin and all evildoers.*

*They will throw them into the fiery furnace, where there will be wailing and grinding of teeth.*[23]

I love how Jesus used parables to get His points across to His followers. In His stories, Jesus used examples and items that were familiar to the people of His times. Thus, the parables were stories with which the people could readily connect to. In telling these parables, Jesus preached the message of God by incorporating the common experiences of the people.

Most of the parables were easy to understand. However, sometimes Jesus told parables which were confusing to many. When He sensed the people may misinterpret His message, He added explanations to His sermons. Many of Jesus' explanation were probably omitted from the final copies of the Gospels.

The Parable of the Wheat and the Weeds was one of the parables that St. Matthew knew would probably confuse most of his readers. So, he decided to include in his book Jesus' explanation of this intriguing story.

Through St. Matthew, Jesus tells us that the wheat and the weeds represent the people of the world: the good people and the not so good people. At the end of the world, on our Final Judgement Day, the Farmer or Harvest Master will come to gather the wheat and the weeds from the field.

The wheat or the good people will be gathered and taken to the heavenly banquet while the weeds or not-so-good people will be gathered and hurled into the fiery furnace.

---

[23]Matthew 13:24-43

The key to understanding this parable is knowing that *only the Harvest Master or the Farmer* will know which are the stalks of wheat and which are the weeds. Only the Harvest Master will be able to decide who has lived according to His Will and who will burn in Hell because they refused to live according to His Will.

As is our human nature, we often try to do the work of the Harvest Master. We often feel the need to point out the weeds from the wheat. We often feel the need to be the ones who pull the weeds from the garden of life. But, that is not our chore. That is not why we have been planted in this earthly garden. We are here to make sure that our stalk of wheat is growing according to God's plan.

It is not our task to say who are weeds and who are wheat. It is not our job to judge the souls of others. *That is God's job.* As my Momma says, "You better leave the judging to God and worry about yourself!" We have enough to do with worrying about our own final destination. We shouldn't be preoccupied with judging other people's souls, trying to decide if they are wheat or weeds. We ought to put our mind on our own business and not in other people's business with God.

Who are we to say if people like the prostitutes in the French Quarter will enter the Kingdom of God? Who are we to say if the rapist or wife beater will be seated at the banquet table? Who are we to say if the drug addict or child abuser will be united with our Creator for all of eternity?

God is the one who will do the saying. Therefore we need to let God be God.

I firmly believe that everyone has a better chance at going to Heaven than going to Hell, anyway. Jesus Christ made sure that the odds were weighted to our sides.

Through His death and resurrection, Jesus provided us with a way to the Father that included the forgiveness of our sins. Thus, anyone who repents of the sins, anyone who confesses to God and His Church, anyone who turns back to the Light of Christ (regardless of their previous sins) will be welcomed at the Father's Banquet Table. That is why we who are merely humans cannot condemn anyone. Even the most heinous of sinners, have been offered salvation through Christ Jesus.

25

The Book of Wisdom assures us that God is indeed a God of Justice.[24] I do believe that all people will get their just rewards in the end. The weeds will definitely be separated from the wheat. But, no mere mortal will be doing the weeding. Only God will stand in judgment of our souls.

One way we can increase our odds of being included in the wheat of Heaven is to make sure that our lives are rooted in the Holy Spirit. For, the Roots of the Spirit run deep into the soil of our earthly dwelling. St. Paul tells us that this same Spirit will intercede on our behalf and that this will nourish and protect our plants of wheat.[25]

It will be through this Spirit that our plants will grow and survive in this earthly pot of weeds. It will also be through this same Spirit that God the Father will be able to read our hearts and know whether or not we truly were members of the living body of Christ.

People of God, just like those little neighbor children who didn't have the ability to tell which of my mother's plants were weeds and which were actual plants, we do not have the ability to tell who of God's creations will enter Heaven and who will be eternally separated from God.

Thus, if we spend our time worrying about those who we think are the weeds in God's Earthly Garden, we will find ourselves missing the life giving-messages of Jesus Christ and protecting nourishment of the Spirit. Jesus came to save the world and not to condemn it. He came to give new life to the plants and not to pull them from His Father's Garden.

Together, let us pray that God's Spirit will indeed nourish our stalks of wheat, giving us new life in Christ. Let us pray that we, the wheat of the Harvest Master,  will be more willing to accept the faults of others and not readily stand in judgment of those faults. And, let us also pray that we and all other sinners of this world will repent of our transgressions so that one day we will be gathered into the arms of the Harvest Master and taken to the Heavenly Banquet.

Children of God's Garden, let us rejoice that we have been chosen to live as God's stalks of wheat amongst the Earth's choking weeds. And, *Rooted in the Spirit*, we cannot be harmed!

---

[24]Wisdom 12:13, 16-19

[25]Romans 8:27

# Feed the Children

While growing up in Uptown New Orleans, I spent most of my childhood years living in a shot-gun double house on Jena Street in the shadows of Our Lady of Lourdes Catholic Church. I always like to talk about where I come from.

I know that much of who I am today is a direct result of where I come from and the folks who were responsible for making sure that I turned out alright!

Back then, I was blessed because I was raised in a house with five parents and six kids. You see, on one side of the shotgun house was my family consisting of my Momma, Daddy and Grand Momma plus my sister, brother and myself. On the other side of the shotgun house lived my Nanny, my Uncle Cyril and their three kids. We were all raised like one big happy family: five parents and six kids.

The two Daddies were hard laborers. My "Pops" was a welder who spent hours upon hours in the heat of New Orleans helping to provide security to homes and ornamental beauty to buildings. My Uncle Cyril was a painter. He worked hard brightening up the houses and businesses of our city.

My Momma was the Business Manager for Martin Wine Cellar. Her job was to make sure that the wine flowed freely and the employees got paid.

My Nanny and My Grand Momma both worked in the Catholic schools as Lunch Ladies. Each day, they headed to one of our elementary schools like Holy Ghost, St. Joan of Arc and St. Raymond, dressed like queens in their dazzling white uniforms, with their heads crowned with beautiful hairnets.

They were responsible for taking care of the children: feeding them, nursing them and loving them in ways that were often taken for granted because they were not the official "Teachers and Counselors" in the schools. But, just like the teachers, my Nanny and Grand Momma played vital roles not only in the kitchens of the Catholic schools, but also in the lives of all the children and their families.

Their job was to feed the hungry each and every day. More often than not, they spent days, proving some of the children with the only balanced meals that they would possibly see on those days.

If it were not for the breakfast and lunch programs that they labored to provide, many of the kids would have gone hungry and become malnourished. In a very real way, their roles as cooks and later for my Nanny as a Cafeteria Manager were more than just a job. It was their ministry. It was their Calling from God. It was their Vocation!

On raining days, they had to feed the kids.
On hot August mornings, they had to feed the kids.
On cold winter afternoons, they had to feed the children.

No matter what was happening at home, in the city or in the world, they knew that they had to be at school, often arriving before sunrise, to make sure that someone was there to feed the gifts of God who would walk through the doors.

It wasn't just their jobs, it was their ministry. It was their Vocation!

In the Gospel written by our Brother Matthew, we hear of a day when Jesus also had to feed the children.

> *When Jesus heard of it, he withdrew in a boat to a deserted place by himself. The crowds heard of this and followed him on foot from their towns. When he disembarked and saw the vast crowd, his heart was moved with pity for them, and he cured their sick.*
>
> *When it was evening, the disciples approached him and said, "This is a deserted place and it is already late; dismiss the crowds so that they can go to the villages and buy food for themselves."*
>
> *(Jesus) said to them, "There is no need for them to go away; give them some food yourselves."*
>
> *But they said to him, "Five loaves and two fish are all we have here."*
>
> *Then he said, "Bring them here to me," and he ordered the crowds to sit down on the grass. Taking the five loaves and the two fish, and looking up to heaven, he said the blessing, broke the loaves, and gave them to the disciples, who in turn gave them to the crowds.*

*They all ate and were satisfied, and they picked up the fragments left over - - twelve wicker baskets full.*

*Those who ate were about five thousand men, not counting women and children.*[26]

When I read this passage, I thought about all those mornings on which my Nanny and Grand Momma had to get up and head to a cafeteria to cook for their children.

No matter what might have been happening in their lives, no matter what the weather was like, they headed out each morning, religiously, to cook for and feed the children of God.

In this Gospel episode, Jesus and His disciples took time to feed the people of God. Although they had more in their natural cafeteria than my Nanny had at St. Raymond Catholic School, they basically had the same task to face. They had to feed the hungry and minister to the needy. And like those cold or rainy days, they had to do it on a day on which many would have decided to not go to work.

You see, on the day that Jesus and His disciples fed the multitudes, they had just found out that the great Prophet John the Baptist had been murdered by Herod's people.

Upon hearing the news that His cousin, John was dead, Jesus wanted to just get away from everybody and spend time in prayer and morning. So, He withdrew in a boat to a deserted place to be by Himself.

We can only imagine how heavy His heart had to be.

John was His cousin, His contemporary and His friend. John was the last of the great prophets. John was the one who announced to the world that The Reign of God was at Hand because the Lamb of God was walking in our midst.

John was Jesus' cousin; someone that Jesus loved like a brother. And, now He was dead.

So, Jesus withdrew to spend time alone in prayer; dealing with the death of His loved one.

---

[26]Matthew 14:13-21

29

But, the people of God followed Him, yearning to be filled by His love and His wisdom. They followed Him , not knowing about His grief and pain. They followed Him, not know about His families loss. They followed Him because they need Him to share with them *"words of everlasting life."*[27]

Jesus understood that even though He was dealing with His own pain, He still needed to minister to His people. This was His Ministry. This was His Calling. This was His Vocation.

Although probably He wanted to take the day off, He knew that both His Heavenly Father and His Followers needed Him to still minister to the Faithful.

God the Father needed His only Begotten Son to be the instrument through which the words of the Prophet Isaiah could be fulfilled. The Father needed Jesus to be the provider for which Isaiah proclaimed,

> *"All you who are thirsty, come to the water!*
> *You who have no money, come, receive grain and eat;*
> *Come, without paying and without cost"*[28]

Although Jesus could have easily taken the day off, God the Father needed Him to be the Life-Giving Water that was promised by Isaiah. He needed Jesus to be the grain that was provided to the people of God, without cost.

Jesus couldn't take the day off, because, the Father needed Him to feed the babies that were knocking on God's Cafeteria Door.

Although Jesus was dealing with the death of his close family member, He did not walk away from His Vocation from God. He ministered to His people, even when He had a valid reason to stop for a while.

In his Letter to the Romans, St. Paul offers us the assurance that nothing can or will stop Christ from loving and providing for us.

In asking the question, *"What will separate us from the Love of Christ?,"*[29] Paul immediately gives the answer.

---

[27]John 6:68

[28]Isaiah 55:1

[29]Romans 8:35

*"Will anguish, or distress, or persecution, or famine, or nakedness, or peril, or the sword? . . .*

*No, in all these things we conquer overwhelmingly through Him who loved us. For I am convinced that neither death, nor life, nor angels, nor principalities, nor present things, nor future things, nor powers, nor height, nor depth, nor any other creature will be able to separate us from the love of God in Christ Jesus our Lord."*[30]

Nothing can separate us from the Love of God. Nothing can stop Jesus from loving us and wanting to feed us each and every day of our lives. That is why, even the death of His cousin, John, could not stop Jesus from ministering to those who needed Him most.

When the crowd followed Him to a distant place, Jesus put aside His own pain and continued to fulfill His calling from the Father. He and His disciples provided the wisdom and grace for which the people were longing. He not only provided the Wisdom and Grace in words. They also provided them in actions and deeds by miraculously feeding bread and fish to more than 5,000 men, women and children.

*"Neither death, nor life, nor angels, nor principalities,"* could stop Jesus from providing what His people needed. Even when others might give up or walk away, Jesus will be there for us.

My brothers and sisters, with Christ as our Light and our Salvation,[31] there is nothing that we should fear! No one can truly harm the Children of God and the followers of the Savior.

In our time of need, Jesus will indeed protect and feed us just as He provided for the people of His day.

But, the miracle of feeding the 5,000 also tells us that in a very real way, Jesus needs all of us to help Him fulfill His Calling. He needs all of us to help Him feed the hungry and give refreshment to the thirsty. Although He is providing the wheat for the bread, He needs us to bake it and place it before His babies.

---

[30]Romans 53, 37-39

[31]Psalm 27:1

31

In the miracle of feeding the 5,000, Jesus provided the food first from the offering of just two fish and five loaves of bead that was presented by a little boy. From that small gift, all would be nourished. But, we need to realize that it was not Jesus who handed out the food. It was the disciples who physically gave to the people the food that the Lord had provided.

In a very real way, this tells us that we must be the ones through whom Jesus physically feeds the people of our day. We must provide the Wisdom of Christ to His Children. We must provide the Bread of Life to the masses. We must be the faucets through which the life giving waters now flow.

Like the disciples of old, Jesus needs us to provide to others, the very thing that has given us life, time and again. No matter what may be happening in our personal lives, we must provide His love to the World.

In the City of New Orleans, the People of God endured what we hope was our darkest hours. Hurricane Katrina was indeed one of the most devastating times of our lives. I know that for me, I can truly testify that neither anguish, nor distress, nor persecution, nor famine, nor nakedness, nor peril, nor the sword can conquer the Will of God.

Like many, I have experienced all of these things as a result of the aftermath of both natural and man made destruction from that deadly hurricane.

But, I can also testify to the fact that if you stay true to your Calling, God will handle all of the adversities that may come your way.

For, like Paul, *"I am convinced that neither death, nor life, nor angels, nor principalities, nor present things, nor future things, nor powers, nor height, nor depth, nor any other creature will be able to separate us from the love of God in Christ Jesus our Lord."*[32]

Now, more than ever, God needs us to be His Disciples.

God needs all of us, not just the Priests, Deacons, Seminarians, Religious Sisters and Religious Brothers, but everyone in the pews to be the one who carry the baskets of bread and fish to His starving people.

---

[32]Romans 8:38-39

He needs us to carry the Baskets of Hope to the children.

He needs us to carry the Baskets of Gratitude to the elderly.

He needs us to carry the Baskets of Care to the sick.

He needs us to carry the Baskets of Comfort to the grieving.

He needs us to carry the Baskets of Forgiveness to the sinners.

He needs us to carry the Baskets of Love to the forgotten.

God needs all of us to be the one who carry the baskets of care to all those who hunger and thirst for righteousness. Today, God calls all of us to be the bearers of His love just as the Angels and Saints have carried those very same baskets for us.

When my Nanny retired from the school system, I had the joy of "saying a few words" at the retirement dinner for all of the Food Services Workers who were bringing their school journey to a close. I thanked them for the ministry that they provided to our children for many decades of years. I also thanked them for the sacrifices that they made to make sure that no child went hungry or thirsty. In a very real way, they were and are the Disciples who carried the baskets of bread to the thousands who came to listen to the Lord and to be fed.

Today, may God allow you to see where He needs to take His Baskets of Love.

Your task is to take and bring what you receive from Jesus back into the world so that everyone will know that nothing can separate us from the Love of God!

May God bless you in Abundance for the Bread and Fish
that you provide to His Children.

Amen

(A Special Note to my Nanny, Mrs. Felicie Honore Coulon: Thank you for your ministry to the children back then. And, thank you for your ministry to me now as my House Keeper and Cook!)

# Momma Loves You!

Throughout the almost 45 years of my life, I have received many types of Christmas gifts: some good and some not so good. Need I mention the six-pack of tube socks that I got from my Aunt Susie Ricard when I was about 10 years old?[33] However, most Christmases were very very good for me.

Since I became a Priest and Pastor, Christmas has always brought to me a bountiful harvest. For Christmas of 2008, I have received a New Orleans Saints neon lamp, custom made floor mats with my KnightTime Ministries logo, a beautiful walking cane from Africa, and loads of Pralines Candies from several parishioners. Indeed, it was a very good year.

But, as good as the Harvest of Christmas '08 was, it will never compare to the Harvest of 1990's Christmas Day. You see, that was the year that I entered the seminary. And Christmas that year is a Christmas that I will always remember.

Now, thinking back, I know that my brother and sister each gave me something. But, I can't remember what their gifts were. And, my friends probably gave me something, too. But, I don't remember their gifts either. What I do remember is the gift that my Momma gave me. It has been a gift that I have cherished from the moment she gave it to me.

On Christmas Morning of 1990, my Mom decided that she would give me something that was more valuable than anything she could have purchased. On that Christmas morning, she sat down and wrote a heartfelt letter to her baby boy. It was something she had never done before.

> In the letter, she told me how proud she was of me. In one part, she wrote, "Mama loves you and appreciates you, and is so proud she can't hold it in. Not because God and you decided to become a priest, but because you are you. Long before the decision was made, I knew you were special . . .Believe, I will always be there for you, no matter what the future holds."

---

[33]I always take the opportunity to remind everyone that SOCKS are not appropriate Christmas gifts for 10 year olds! *Rock'em Sock'em Robots* or a *G.I. Joe with a Kung-Fu Grip* would have been more appropriate. I assure you that my Aunt Susie and her husband, Uncle Glenn Ricard, have learned this valuable lesson simply by virtue of how many times I have told this story!

I don't know if she realized then, how much this letter would mean to me. In this gesture of her maternal love, I am forever reminded of how much her love has empowered me to be me.

Indeed, her love has been empowering me through the many events in my life.

When we look at the life of Christ, we can find a time when God, the Father, told the world how proud that He was of His Son, Jesus. In the works of our Brother Luke, God affirms His Son before the world as His Boy began His public Ministry.

In the Gospel of Luke, we read,

> *The people were filled with expectation, and all were asking in their hearts whether John might be the Messiah. John answered them all, saying, "I am baptizing you with water, but one mightier than I is coming. I am not worthy to loosen the thongs of his sandals. He will baptize you with the Holy Spirit and fire. His winnowing fan is in his hand to clear his threshing floor and to gather the wheat into his barn, but the chaff he will burn with unquenchable fire."*
>
> *Exhorting them in many other ways, He preached good news to the people.*
>
> *Now Herod the tetrarch, who had been censured by Him because of Herodias, his brother's wife, and because of all the evil deeds Herod had committed, added still another to these by (also) putting John in prison.*
>
> *After all the people had been baptized and Jesus also had been baptized and was praying, heaven was opened and the Holy Spirit descended upon Him in bodily form like a Dove. And a voice came from Heaven, "You are My beloved Son; with You I am well pleased."* [34]

This is one of many empowering moments in Jesus' life, but this one is particularly significant.

---

[34]Luke 3:15-22

Just as my Momma's letter came only a few months after I started the seminary, this affirmation from God the Father happened at the beginning of Jesus' public ministry. And, on that special day that Jesus was baptized by His cousin John, the Holy Spirit descended and filled His Heart with the grace-filled message of the Father: *"Jesus, Daddy, loves You."*

With this always resonating in His heart, Jesus lived an earthly life that echoed the love that He shared with His Father. He proclaims this love by telling His disciples, *"As the Father loves Me; so I also love you."*[35] Throughout the Gospels, we hear of how Jesus draws on His love from the Father and passes it on to all in He meets.

At the moment of His Baptism we hear the words from Heaven, *"You are My beloved Son; with You I am well pleased"* or as another translation put it, *"You are My Beloved Son. On You My favor rests."* In this, the Creator was telling His Baby Boy, "It's not what You do that makes Me love You, it is Who You are." The Father does not say, *"This Is My Beloved Son, Who does things I am proud of."* He says, *"You are My beloved Son; with You I am well pleased"* Or paraphrased into our times, the Father was telling Jesus, *"Daddy loves You and appreciates You, and is so proud . . .because You are You."*

At His Baptism, Jesus is affirmed at the very core of His being, simply for being Himself in a loving relation with the Father. Later, we learn that this relationship would become known to us as the Third Person in the Holy Trinity: The Holy Spirit. For, the Spirit of God is the manifestation of the love between the Father and the Son.

Through the Holy Spirit, the vehicle of God's love for us, we are challenged to stop estimating our own worth by what we do or what we possess. God's unconditional love challenges us to realize that we are worthy of the best simply because we are who we are.

The affirming love that the Father proclaimed at Jesus' Baptism is expressed in the public ministry of Our Lord. Immediately after John baptized Him, Jesus went off to the desert and was faced with the temptations of Satan. Having heard his Father's voice, He knew that He had the power to say, "no," to Satan. And in saying no to Satan, and affirming the Father's love, He returned from the desert even more powerful. He immediately began preaching the Good News and healing the sick, proclaiming that the Kingdom of God was at hand.

---

[35]John 15:9

My brothers and sister, as we are loved by God, our Father, so too must we love one another. We have important work to do in building each other up with affirming messages of love. Our work is to write continual Love Letters to each other.

It is love that empowers people to do good, to live in peace and harmony, to stand against what needs to be changed. Those who show love actually show God, the Holy Spirit, to others.

Like my Momma and God, our Father, all parents have a special vocation to love. It is the whisper of "I love you" from the earliest moments of infancy through the years of childhood that builds the foundation of a loving personality.

Parents need to devote themselves to planting the seeds of love daily in the hearts of their children. For, a child without that early sense of being loved and accepted will find the struggles of adult life to be almost insurmountable obstacles.

Wives and husbands are vowed to love one another in a unique way. It is the people that we are closest to, whom we can empower the most through our own selfless, loving acts and affirming, life-giving presence.

We are challenged daily to put aside the nonessentials, the petty struggles, and to plunge after the love that is the source of our life. For, in this love we find God. No one has been forgotten by God; thus, everyone is called to love in return.

But, *"Love Thy Neighbor"* [36]is easier said than done.

Yet, when we our active practice is the practice of love, we build up the people around us and help them to relate to God, the Author of Love. In doing so, it becomes easier and easier for us and them to truly live in a "Love Thy Neighbor" Spirit.

The empowering love of God works hard to take us outside our comfort zones. For, the deepest awareness of true love helps us to understand the fundamental unity of all peoples. When we see fellow humans suffering, the Father's love for us challenges us to do something about it. Whether it be something direct and charitable, or whether it be work to make the political systems of the world more just. Or both.

---

[36]Luke 10:27

Children of God, we are called to love one another, to offer reconciliation to each other, to offer peace to all. In this loving unity, we are empowered together by the love of our God, by the love that is our God.

Today, through the Blood of the Lamb, Jesus' Daddy says to us, *"I, the Lord, have called you for the Victory of Justice, I have grasped you by the hand."*[37]

May you have the courage to reach up and grasp the outstretched hand of the Redeemer, and know that you are loved.


Today, God the Father says to us,
*"Daddy loves you and appreciates you, and is so proud*
*. . . (Not because of something you do,)*
           *because you are you."*

Amen.

**A Motherly Hug**
**The night before Fr. Tony was ordained**
**May 26, 1995**

---

[37]Isaiah 42:6

# The Things Our Momma Taught Us

For most adults, when we look back on our lives and all the years we spent as children in our parents' homes, we can credit our Mother for the many wonderful and wisdom-filled things we have learned about life. For most of us, our Moms and our mother figures, were the ones we went to when we really needed to learn about life.

In reflecting on the gift of our Mothers, I thought I would share with you some of the great lessons that flow from the mouths of Mothers.

Not too long ago, I received a wonderful email from a friend that included a list called, "The Things Our Momma Taught Us."

In the email, the list read:

Our Moms taught us TO APPRECIATE A JOB WELL DONE
- by saying, "If you're going to kill each other, do it outside -
I just mopped the floor!"

Our Moms taught us about RELIGION
- by saying, "You better pray that
that Kool Aid comes out of my carpet."

Our Moms taught us about TIME TRAVEL
- by saying, "If you keep it up, I'm going to knock you
into the middle of next week!"

Our Moms taught us LOGIC
- by saying, "Because I said so, that's why."

Our Moms taught us to have FORESIGHT
- by saying, "Make sure you wear clean underwear,
in case you're in an accident."

Our Moms taught us about MEDICINE
- by saying, "If you keep making that face, it's gonna stick like that!"

Our Moms taught us about HUMOR
- by saying, "When that lawn mower cuts off your toes,
don't come running to me."

Our Moms taught us about IRONY
>- by saying, "Do you want me to give you something to cry for?"

Our Moms taught us about ANTICIPATION
>- by saying, "Oh, you can act a fool, now,
>> but, just wait till we get home!"

Our Moms taught us about the WEATHER
>- by saying, "Clean this up, It looks like a tornado just hit this room."

Our Moms taught us about my ROOTS
>- by saying, "Close the door: Do you think you were born in a barn?"

Our Moms taught us about GENETICS
>- by saying, "You act just like your Paw!"

Our Moms taught us about BEHAVIOR MODIFICATION
>- by saying, "Stop acting like your father!"

Our Moms taught us about ENVY
>- by saying, "There are millions of children in the world
>> who wish they had the great parents that you have!"

Our Moms taught us about the WISDOM of AGE
>- by saying, "When you get to be my age, you will understand."

And, my all-time favorite -
Our Moms taught us about LONGEVITY, GOD'S GRACE and JUSTICE
>- by saying, "I hope that I live long enough to see God bless you
>> with children that are JUST like YOU!"

I don't know about you, but, I have truly learned a lot from my Momma!

In Chapter 10 of the Gospel according to our Brother John, Jesus describes His relationship with us as that of a Good Shepherd.[38] In describing Himself in such a protective role, Jesus describes Himself just as a Mother would describe her relationship with her children.

---

[38]John 10:11

Jesus says,

> *"I am the Good Shepherd. A good shepherd lays down his life for the sheep. A hired man, who is not a shepherd and whose sheep are not his own, sees a wolf coming and leaves the sheep and runs away, and the wolf catches and scatters them.*
>
> *This is because he works for pay and has no concern for the sheep. I am the good shepherd, and I know mine and mine know me, just as the Father knows me and I know the Father; and I will lay down my life for the sheep.* "[39]

Like many mothers, Jesus recognized His role as protector, nurturer and guide for the those whom God put in His care. He is the Good Shepherd: the one who is responsible for defending the flock, no matter what. As our Good Shepherd, Jesus is willing to do whatever it takes to make sure that we turn-out alright. Even if it means He has to literally, "lay down His life for His sheep."

In most families, the mother is called to do the same thing, to do whatever it takes to protect the sheep that God has gracefully blessed her with. Even if it literally means she has to *lay down her life* for her sheep.

As the Good Shepherd, Jesus already knows what we need and has worked extremely hard to provide it for us. He also know that ultimately, His role as Shepherd is to lead His Flock to the Eternal Paradise that is the Kingdom of Heaven.

Our faith tells us that Jesus, our Good Shepherd, has already cleared the pathway to that Eternal Paradise. He did it by taking upon His back, all of our sins, carrying them to the Hill of Calvary, dying on a tree, and three days later, shattering the walls of a tomb that once was able to hold the sheep bound.

Through the Life, Death and Resurrection of Jesus Christ, our Good Shepherd, the pearly gates that lead into the Green Pastures of Heaven have been flung open and our arrival time has been set.

It is now up to us to follow His lead and ultimately *"enter the temple gates with praise, its courts with thanksgiving."*[40]

---

[39] John 10:11-15

[40] Psalm 100:4

41

As we reflect on the gift of our Mothers, most of us feel blessed because God so readily chose these women to be our Mothers. It was because of God's Love, that we were presented as precious gifts to them. It was because of God's Love, that we were cared for and protected by them. It was because of God's Love, that we know not only our Mother's Love but the love of many women who have served as Mothers to us in more ways than just giving birth to us.

For, God's Love for us is so great that He would stop at nothing to make sure that we turn out alright! That's why he sent me my Momma!

As I look back on my life, I realize that I have learned a great deal of stuff from my Mother, from her wise statements to her life examples of perseverance and prayer. But, I guess that the greatest lesson that I have learned from her is that being her child is NOT the best thing that has ever happened to me. The greatest lesson that she taught me was, the lesson that we are given in the First Letter of St. John: *"Beloved: See what love the Father has bestowed on us that we may be called the children of God."*[41]

You see, my brothers and sisters, the greatest lesson that a Mother can teach her child is the fact that though you might belong to her on Earth, ultimately, you belong to God. You are God's Beloved Son. You are God's Beloved Daughter. And, as such, OUR Father in Heaven is preparing a place for us that will multiply by a hundredfold the love of our homes on earth. That's why He sent the Good Shepherd. That's why He gave us loving Mothers. So that one day, we will be made ready to enter our Heavenly Home and be fully nurtured by God, Our Heavenly Father.

One day, a little girl was sitting and watching her mother do the dishes at the kitchen sink when she suddenly noticed that her mother had several strands of white hair sticking out in contrast to her beautiful brunette hair. So, she looked at her mother and curiously asked, "Momma, why are some of your hairs white?"

Seizing the moment to teach her daughter a valuable lesson, the mother replied "Well, every time that you do something wrong and make me cry or unhappy, one of my hairs turns white." Looking curious again, the little girl replies, "Is that why ALL of your Momma's hairs are white?"

May the Lord bless us and our Mommas.

---

[41] 1 John 3:1

# Pictures of My Momma

**Mr. and Mrs. Rodney Joseph Ricard**
**April 15, 1961**

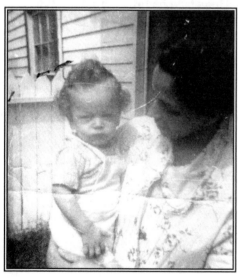

**Baby Tony and His Momma**
**1965**

**Young Tony and**
**His Momma - July 1982**

**Fr. Tony's Family on the night before
he was ordained to the Priesthood
May 26, 1995**

**Fr. Tony and His Momma
in the River Jordan - Israel 1996**

# SECTION TWO
## Lessons from Jesus

# The Crucifix
## Our Lady Star of the Sea Church

# Do You Love Me?

*The Love Boat Theme*

Love, exciting and new
Come aboard, we're expecting you.
And, love, life's sweetest reward,
Let it float, it floats back to you.

The Love Boat soon will be making another run.
The Love Boat promises something for everyone.
Set a course for adventure,
your mind on a new romance.
And love won't hurt anymore.
It's an open smile on a friendly shore.

Welcome Aboard - It's Love..........
The Love Boat.
The Love Boat.
It's love. It's love.[42]

In my younger days, I loved watching *The Love Boat* on television. That show seems to be a TV Show that will never go away. Most of us know that *The Love Boat* was an immediate hit back in 1977 when it debuted. The show featured a cast of regular characters that seemed to either fall in love with someone new every week or end up in some type of trouble every week.

From Gopher, the Yeoman-Purser, who was always cooking up stupid schemes to "get over" on the captain, to Isaac Washington, the Ship's Bartender, who always seems to know the answers to everyone's love problems. Although, he never had a regular girlfriend on the show.

Part of what made the Love Boat a great success was not only the antics of its regular crew, it was also the parade of major TV and Movie Stars that showed-up for the cruise each week. On the show, big stars like Gene Kelly, Tom Hanks, and Vanessa Williams all appeared. But, my favorite star who seemed to show up almost every year was Charo (the *Cuchie Cuchie* Girl) from the 1970's. Indeed, now that there is late night cable television, *The Love Boat* will sail on for many more years.

---

[42]*The Love Boat* theme song was sung by Jack Jones. The lyrics were written by Paul Williams with music by Charles Fox.

Just as *The Love Boat* helped the entire nation learn more about falling in love, the Bible helps the entire world understand how to better be people of love. In fact, The Bible really is a big Love Letter from God. In Sacred Scripture, God tells us just how much He loves us and how we should respond to that love.

That is why in summing up His messages to us, Jesus simply says, "This is my commandment: love one another as I love you. No one has greater love than this, to lay down one's life for one's friends."[43] Simply put, our expected response to God's offer of love is to share that love with all we meet.

In the First Letter of Saint John, we read, *"See what love the Father has bestowed on us that we may be called the Children of God."*[44] In this, we are called to remember that God loves us so much that He has not only claimed us as His subjects. He has bestowed upon us the title of *Children of God.* That means that in the Eyes of God, although we are created beings, we have been elevated by the love of Christ to a new level of creation and are destined to be with God in the New Eden that is the Kingdom of Heaven.

But, we cannot take our lofty positions for granted. Just because we have been promised a place at the Banquet Feast in Heaven doesn't mean that we can live our lives in any manner that we choose. We are called to give an active and obvious response to God's love.

> *"Beloved, let us love one another, because love is of God;*
> *everyone who loves is begotten by God and knows God.*
> *Whoever is without love does not know God, for God is love.*
> *In this way the love of God was revealed to us: God sent His*
> *only Son into the world so that we might have life through Him.*
>
> *In this is love: not that we have loved God, but that He loved us*
> *and sent His Son as expiation for our sins. Beloved, if God so*
> *loved us, we also must love one another.*
>
> *No one has ever seen God. Yet, if we love one another, God*
> *remains in us, and His love is brought to perfection in us."*[45]

---

[43]John 15:12-13

[44]1 John 3:1

[45]1 John 4:7-12

It is only when that love reaches perfection that we will get our chance to see God face to face.

One of my most favorite scripture passages is found in the Chapter 21 of the Gospel of John. In this particular passage, we get a glimpse of an earlier version of *The Love Boat*. But, rather than it being a boat filled with folks searching for "a love mate," it was a boat filled with men who were still trying to figure out how to continue loving and serving Jesus even though He had been crucified by the civil authorities. Chapter 21 is the final Chapter in the Gospel of John and describes the final appearance that the Risen Lord made to Apostles.

As the men of pure love fished, Jesus the Man of Divine Love appeared to them. In this, His third appearance to His beloved followers, Jesus first shared breakfast with them and then taught St. Peter the greatest lesson of love.

In this lesson, Jesus asked St. Peter a simple question, *"Do you love Me?"*

> *"Simon, son of John, do you love Me more than these?"*
> *He said to Him, "Yes, Lord, You know that I love You."*
> *He said to him, "Feed My lambs."*
>
> *He then said to him a second time, "Simon, son of John, do You love Me?" He said to Him, "Yes, Lord, You know that I love You." He said to him, "Tend My sheep."*
>
> *He said to him the third time, "Simon, son of John, do you love Me?" Peter was distressed that He had said to him a third time, "Do you love Me?" and he said to Him,*
> *"Lord, You know everything; You know that I love You."*
> *(Jesus) said to him, "Feed My sheep.*
>
> *Amen, amen, I say to you, when you were younger, you used to dress yourself and go where you wanted; but when you grow old, you will stretch out your hands, and someone else will dress you and lead you where you do not want to go."*
>
> *He said this signifying by what kind of death he would glorify God. And when He had said this, He said to him, "Follow Me."*[46]

---

[46]John 21:15-19

Some believe that this episode of love was Jesus' way of saying to Peter, "I forgive you for denying me." That's why Jesus asked three times, *"Do you love Me?"* Remember, Simon Peter had denied Him three times before the crucifixion.

What I loved about this interchange between Jesus and the First Pope, is the fact that every time Peter said, *"Yes, Lord, You know I love You,"* Jesus gave him a simple command.

*"Feed My lambs." "Tend My sheep." "Feed My sheep."*

In the end, Jesus simply says to Peter, *"Follow Me!"*

In other words, *"Respond to My Love by Loving others!"*

You know, when I was in elementary school, back when the Love Boat first came on television, we used to write little love letters to some of the girls in class. And at the end of the letter, we would do that old elementary thing in order to get a response from the girl. We would draw two boxes at the end and write, "Do you love me check yes; check no."

That was always the best way to find out if the girl would be your girlfriend. "Do you love me, check yes; check no." And of course, for me, they always checked, "yes." (Who could blame them?)

Well, I believe God, He too concluded *His Love Letter* to us in the same way we used to conclude our love letters in elementary school. You see, this episode between Jesus and Saint Peter, actually comes from the last chapter of the Fourth Book of the Gospel. Essentially, God ends His love-filled writings to us, by asking St. Peter and us, "Do we love Him?"

And like an elementary school boy, God is also is waiting for a response:

We either need to check "Yes" or check "No!"

You see, when he asks us "Do we love Him?" If we answer by saying yes, then we must be like Peter and respond by "Feeding His Lambs" and "Tending His Sheep."

That's how we will show God that we have indeed checked "Yes" as we respond to His love.

49

Like with St. Peter, God needs all who love Him to take care of the folks around us. That might mean, feeding the homeless, giving to the poor, or even laying down your life for Him by becoming a priest, a deacon, a Religious Sister or a Religious Brother.

But, it also goes farther than that. Checking "Yes" also means seeing your family and friends as God's Sheep. Taking care of your loved ones, your children, your parents and your friends, as God has called you to do.

Today, God asks each of us, "Do you love Me? Check yes; check no."

You know, I believe that the greatest gift that God has ever given us on Earth is the life of His Son. The next great gift He will give us is entrance into Heaven. But, to get in, He is going to be looking for how we responded to all that He has written in His *Love Letter* to us. He's going to check to see if we checked "Yes" or checked "No" by seeing if we loved one another as He has loved us.

You know, The Love Boat series ended in May of 1986. Though it may live on during late-night reruns, the Love Boat will never really sail, again. And, that's OK.

Because, the boat that we need to really be concentrating on is the boat that will cross the River of Death and take us to the Kingdom of Heaven. Oh, the Love Boat may have sailed to Cancun and the Bahamas, nice little paradises on Earth. But, the Boat that Captain Jesus drives will take us to a Paradise that will surpass anything we can ever experience here.

So, as one of the church's First Mates, in the name of Jesus I say, I say to you:

Love, exciting and new
    Come aboard, He's expecting you.
And, love, life's sweetest reward,
    Let it float, it floats back to you.

Our Savior soon will be making another run.
Our Savior promises salvation to everyone.
    Set a course for the Kingdom,
    your mind on a new romance.

Come and experience Love. . .

Amen

# Running From the Bear

Once there were two friends walking through the woods. When suddenly, a bear came up behind them. Well, as they walked faster, one of the friends reached into his gym bag and pulled out his brand new pair of high flying basketball shoes.

As they walked forward, he began to put on his new shoes and to tie them really tight. The other guy looked down at him and said, *"Why are you putting on those shoes? You'll never out run that bear."*

And his friend looked up and said, "I don't have to outrun that bear. *I only have to out run you!"*

My Brothers and Sisters in Christ, more often than not, our relationships with others can be quite confusing. Sometimes we are those doting, loving friends that can't do enough to help those we love. And then, sometimes we are like that guy with the brand new basketball shoes: only thinking of our own survival and not really having concern for others.

God calls us to look at how we relate with others: How we relate to God? How we relate to our neighbors? And, how we relate with ourselves. Simply put, as followers of Jesus Christ, *"Do we really love as we should?"*

Jesus came to teach us about love, Love of God, Love of our Neighbors and Love of Ourselves. In fact, sharing Love was at the core of Jesus' mission on Earth. He came to teach us that love is the way of the Father. It is the way to salvation, to joy and to true happiness.

In the Gospel of our Brother Matthew, Jesus tells us that God's primary commandment to us is to Love.

> *When the Pharisees heard that He had silenced the Sadducees, they gathered together, and one of them [a scholar of the law] tested Him by asking, "Teacher, which commandment in the law is the greatest?" He said to him, "You shall love the Lord, your God, with all your heart, with all your soul, and with all your mind. This is the greatest and the first commandment. The second is like it: You shall love your neighbor as yourself."* [47]

---

[47]Matthew 22:34-49

In breaking down this passage from Matthew's Gospel, we are faced with three levels of true love.

The first level is Loving God.
The second level is Loving our Neighbors.
The third level is the Loving Ourselves.

Each of the levels of love are really dependant on the other levels. That is why we can better understand this scripture passage, by reflecting on each of them in reverse order. First, we should examine the love that we have for ourselves. Then, we can see how that love connects us to others and ultimately to our God.

Each of us must ask ourselves, "Do I love myself?"

In loving who and what I am,
> Do I respect myself?
> Do I admire myself?
> Do I see myself in the image of God?
> Do I see myself as good?

"Do I love myself?"

Many of us have difficulty loving ourselves. Sometimes difficulties come from the pains and heartache that we have endured in life. Many times, we allow the outside world to cloud our inner beauty and prevent us from seeing just how precious we really are.

In fact, because of the stuff that the world throws at us, we will spend a great deal of time tearing ourselves apart. Often we do this by comparing ourselves to others.

My hair isn't like hers. My eyes aren't like his. I wish I could work hard like her. I wish I was as smart as him. We simply fall into the trap of using others as the model on which we judge ourselves. Although we have all been beautifully made, we can begin to believe that we are not the awesome creations that God has made in His images and likeness.

We begin to have false images of whom we really are. We fail to really see and love ourselves as the blessings that God made us to be.

In all of this, we must stop and say, "I love myself!"

We can't allow ourselves to tear ourselves apart.

Part of self-love is found in accepting that none of us are perfect. We all have impurities and limitations and we are all are sinners. In recognizing that, we can come to know our true selves. But, it's in knowing our true selves that we can truly come to love who we are and why we were made.

Once I have dealt with my love for myself, then, and only then, can I truly share that love with another person. Jesus said we must love our neighbor as we love ourselves. But, if I do not love myself, how can I love others?

In focusing on our love for others, we all know that we would be miserable individuals if we were not joined in loving relationships with others. Good friends help us to know that God loves us. But, we must realize that friends are people, too. We can hurt our relationships with our friends by forgetting that they have feelings and needs just like we do. Therefore, just as we must protect and love ourselves, we must protect and love others.

We also have to figure out who are our true friends and who are those false friends that lurk in our lives. A true friend is one on whom we can depend. One who will be with us in happiness and in sadness. False friends are those who are looking out for only themselves. We have all experienced people who think only about what they can get out of a situation.

In looking at how we love our friends, we also have to look at how we love and treat our family.

What is our relationship like with our spouse, children or siblings?

We know that we love them, but do we really show it? Do we ever let them know how much they mean to us? Even when we have those knock down, drag-out fights, we still know that we love them. And, have we realized that they are real people too?

After examining our relationships with ourselves and with others, we can then turn our eyes on our relationship with God.

What is my relationship with God?
>How do I see God?
>Do I really feel that God loves me?

The Bible says that God created a covenant with Abraham and Moses and fulfilled that covenant through Jesus. For in Jesus, God showed the depth of love by dying for us. In John 3:16, we read, *"For God so loved the world that He gave His only Son, so that everyone who believes in Him might not perish but might have eternal life."*[48]

That means that God's love for us is so deep that He would stop at nothing to save us. His love for us is both unending and unconditional. That is why Psalm 145 tells us, *"The LORD is gracious and merciful, slow to anger and abounding in love. The LORD is good to all, compassionate to every creature."*[49]

Most of all, God is always a God of forgiveness?

Therefore, you need to ask yourself, "What is my relationship with God like? Have I developed a personal relationship that allows me the simple ability to sit and talk with God?"

Once we have analyzed our relationships with ourselves, our neighbors and God, we have to take steps to allow those relationships to grow. Here are three steps which can help develop those relationships.

First:
If You Love Somebody...
> *You must communicate with them.*

You have to think within yourself about who and what your are.
You have to be willing to talk to you friends and trust that they will be willing to share with you.
You also have to take time to talk to God by developing a prayer life that allows you to spend time with God. As you know, communicating with God can come in many forms of prayer: singing, dancing, speaking and in art.

Second:
If You Love Somebody...
> *You must take time to learn more about them.*

Everything changes. We change, people change, and how we see God also changes. Although God never changes, how we see Him does.

---

[48]John 3:16

[49]Psalm 145:8-9

Therefore, we need to take time to learn about what we really like, what our friends really like and what God desires for us. Through talking and studying, we can learn more about God, others and ourselves.

Third:
If You Love Somebody...
    *You must do something special for them....even if it's not your cup of tea!*

You also should do special things for yourself. Everyone deserves to treat themselves to something every now and then. (But not all the time.)

Love and friendship is a partnership. That means that you have to share a mutual willingness to do things your friends like.

You should also do something special for God. Saying the Rosary, saying a special prayer, observing Lenten Fasts and Abstinence, arriving early for Sunday Mass and staying until it is over, taking time to say, "Thank You Lord for all you have given me," are all ways of doing special things for God.

If you can do these three things, your love for yourself, for you neighbors and for God will grow in leaps and bounds. But, you must be willing to allow it to grow.

Love must be the basis of our relationships with everything. It must be the basis of our relationship with ourselves and our neighbors. And it definitely must be the basis for our relationship with our God. Once we realize that, we will indeed, begin to see the world differently and will treat all of God's creatures differently.

I guess that if Jesus was one of those men running away from the bear, and He realized that He had a brand new pair of basketball shoes in His gym bag, He would have probably offered His new shoes to His friend.

Anyway, He was Jesus. And, Lord knows, anyone who could walk on water could surely out run the average bear.

---

*Some friends bring ruin on us,*

*but a true friend is more loyal than a brother.*

Proverbs 18:24

# I Mean to Stay at Your House

As a teenager, I attended St. Augustine High School[50] in New Orleans, Louisiana. While as a student there, I actively participated in many school organizations. I was a class president, the yearbook editor, the City's high school representative on Mayor Ernest "Dutch" Morial's Mardi Gras Task Force, and an American Legion's delegate to Louisiana Boys State.

Along with many other activities, I also played Xylophone and Tympani in St. Augustine's concert band. However, the activity that I cherished most from my high school years, is my participation in the nationally known marching band, the St. Augustine's Marching 100.

During my years in St. Aug's Marching Band, we were honored to participate in many big events in New Orleans and throughout the South.

We played at many New Orleans Saints Games, performed for President Jimmy Carter (which shows how old I am), played for numerous downtown conventions, and marched in several Mardi Gras Parades.

We even performed at the *1980 Abbeyville Cattle Festival.* (O.K., So the Cattle Festival isn't that big of an event to folks around the nation. But, for the people in Abbeyville, LA, it is.)

Some of our more exciting experiences happened as we marched down the streets of New Orleans in the many major Mardi Gras Parades. No words can truly explain the feelings you have when marching in a parade as a member of the city's most popular high school band.

The excitement in the crowd reaches a fever pitch when St. Aug passes by during a parade. Even before St. Aug reaches your block, there seems to be  an electricity that runs through the crowd. The band could be blocks away and yet people somehow know that the Marching 100 is coming.

It was not uncommon to see people holding up their children so that they might get a good look, as the *Best Band* in the city performed for them. Boyfriends often lifted their girlfriends onto their shoulders so that they might also see the sparkling helmets and those dancing shoes of the Purple Knights.

---

[50]In New Orleans, St. Augustine High School is affectionately known as "St. Aug."

Folks climbed trees and stood on trash cans. Ice-chests became step stools and the beds of pick-up trucks became dance floors. People did whatever they could to *see and hear* the Purple Pride of New Orleans.

No feelings in the world could replace the excitement that most band members had when we saw the joy that our music and performances brought to many on the streets of New Orleans.

For some, the excitement at seeing The Marching 100 was almost a religious experience!

In the Gospel according to our Brother Luke, we hear a similar story of excitement in a city's streets. But, the level of this excitement surpasses even that which accompanies the coming of *St. Augustine's Marching 100.*

In Luke 19:1-10, the excitement in the streets of Jericho was in anticipation of the coming of *Jesus the Nazarean.*

> *At that time, Jesus came to Jericho and intended to pass through the town. Now a man there named Zacchaeus, who was a chief tax collector and also a wealthy man, was seeking to see who Jesus was; but he could not see Him because of the crowd, for he was short in stature. So he ran ahead and climbed a sycamore tree in order to see Jesus, who was about to pass that way. When He reached the place, Jesus looked up and said to him, "Zacchaeus, come down quickly, for today I must stay at your house."*
>
> *And he came down quickly and received Him with joy.*
>
> *Then they all saw this, they began to grumble, saying, "He has gone to stay at the house of a sinner." But Zacchaeus stood there and said to the Lord, "Behold, half of my possessions, Lord, I shall give to the poor, and if I have extorted anything from anyone I shall repay it four times over."*
>
> *And Jesus said to him, "Today salvation has come to this house because this man too is a descendant of Abraham. For the Son of Man has come to seek and to save what was lost."*[51]

---

[51]Luke 19:1-10

57

In this beautiful story of love and forgiveness, we hear that when the town's folk had heard that Jesus was passing through, many of them lined the streets to catch a glimpse of the great healer and preacher about whom so many had been talking.

Zacchaeus, a respected member of the Jericho's upper class, also shared this excitement. Like people waiting to see St. Aug's Marching 100, he wanted to have a good view for seeing Jesus when the Lord passed-by in the streets.

First, he pushed his way to the front of the crowd and tried to get a good spot. But because he was not very tall, he found it hard to really see the Lord.

Spotting a Sycamore Tree along Jesus' route, Zacchaeus climbed up its branches so that he could see over the crowd. There, in the tree, he could see Jesus as He passed below. It was because Zacchaeus climbed that tree that Jesus noticed him and subsequently ate at his house and offered Zacchaeus the gift of salvation.

Though Zacchaeus was a known sinner, Jesus did not refuse to offer him the chance to be saved. For, Jesus was able to see the imperishable spirit which dwelled inside of Zacchaeus.[52] Although he was a sinner, Zacchaeus still had the opportunity to welcome Jesus into his home because of the blessed Spirit which was given to him at the moment of his conception.

In a very real way, Each of us is like Zacchaeus. The arrival of Jesus Christ in our midst breathes an air of hope and excitement into our lives. None of us would want to have our sight of Jesus blocked by a crowd or obstructed by people who do not really care that Jesus is alive.

Each of us wants to make sure that when Jesus returns we have the best seat in the grand stands. A seat where we might clearly see and hear the revelation of Christ's Second Coming.

However, in a very real way, many of us allow our sins to become the crowd that blocks our vision of Christ. Many allow the negative attitudes of others to impede their minds and block their understanding of Christ's ongoing revelations through Creation. Many allow their personal inhibitions to prevent them from doing all that is possible to assure that they will have a good view when Christ comes again.

---

[52]Wisdom 12:1 says, God's "imperishable spirit is in all things!"

Like Zacchaeus, we are all called to find a way to better see Christ in the midst of the crowds that block our paths to Him. Like that Sycamore Tree which grew along the streets of Jericho, there are many sacramental trees offered to us by God, through the Church, which help us to climb up and see over the crowds in our lives.

The Sacrament of Reconciliation, The Sacrament of the Anointing of the Sick, and The Sacrament of the Eucharist are three primary ways that God offers us a grace-filled boost to see over the crowd.

In the Sacrament of Reconciliation, the Sacrament of Penance, we are able to wipe away all of those things which have clouded our view of God's Love for us, God's Love for Others and God's Love for Creation. Through the forgiveness of our sins, we are offered a higher spot on the tree which allows us to see Christ in our midst.

In the Sacrament of the Anointing of the Sick, we are offered mental, spiritual and physical healing which are necessary for us to be able to climb the trees along Christ's route.

In paragraph 1532 of the Catechism of the Catholic Church, we read,

> "The special grace of the sacrament of the Anointing of the Sick has as its effects: the uniting of the sick person to the passion of Christ, for his own good and that of the whole Church; the strengthening, peace, and courage to endure in a Christian manner the sufferings of illness or old age; the forgiveness of sins, if the sick person was not able to obtain it through the sacrament of Penance; the restoration of health, if it is conducive to the salvation of his soul; the preparation for passing over to eternal life."[53]

This tells us that in the Anointing of the Sick, it is possible for our sins to also forgiven. Thus, we are boosted higher on the tree and above the crowd.

In the Sacrament of the Eucharist, we not only experience the arrival of Christ in this, our spiritual home, we have the opportunity to experience the arrival of Christ in our bodies.

---

[53]Catechism of the Catholic Church Section Two: Article Five Paragraph 1532

Zacchaeus not only welcomed Christ into his physical home. He welcomed Christ into his life. In this, he showed us that no crowd can prevent us from seeing and hearing what Jesus has to offer. For, through the Eucharist, Christ offers us a view from within; a view with not external obstructions.

From this interior viewpoint, the questions that we must all ask ourselves are: "Am I willing to be like Zacchaeus and climb a tree to see Jesus?"

"Am I willing to be like Zacchaeus and put aside my public position, to put aside my personal prestige and earthly success, in order to get a better view of the Christ in our midst?"

"Am I willing to do whatever it takes to let Jesus know that I want Him to honor me like He honored Zaccaeus by entering and reclining in my house?"

In a very real way, Jesus is looking at you and me on this very day and saying *"Come down quickly, for today, I must stay at your house."* Knowing that Jesus wants to come home with us today, we must also ask, "Are our houses ready for Jesus to come home with us? Do I need to do some house cleaning before Jesus comes in?"

During a momentary pause in Mardi Gras Parade, it was nothing for someone in the crowd to come up to a member of the Marching 100 and ask if he would mind being in a picture with them. From my four years of marching in St. Aug's band, I must be in hundreds of pictures taken during Mardi Gras Parades (which is good because every home should have at least one picture of me).

I can remember that most of the people taking pictures were tourists. They wanted to take a piece of New Orleans home with them. And what better piece to remember Mardi Gras than a picture with a member of St. Augustine Marching 100: especially a picture with this good-looking member of the band.

Well, in the Eucharist, we not only have the chance to take the memory of Christ back with us and into our homes. *We have the opportunity take Jesus Christ, Himself,* into our homes.

People of God, may we come to realize that in the Eucharist, Jesus is not only passing by on His Route to the heavenly Jerusalem. He is truly present in our midst. May we have the strength to do all that we have to do, to see over the crowds, and to join in the celebration of Christ's arrival: even if it means that we have to climb a sycamore tree to see Him. May we realize that Jesus wants to stay at our houses, today!

# The Coffin Attack!

The other night, my Rottweiler, Pepper, and I were out on an evening stroll. As we walked a block from my rectory, we began to pass the entrance gates to the Historic St. Roch Cemetery. Now, normally, I won't walk past those gates at night. I am easily scared! But, for some reason, Pepper wanted to head in that direction.

As we passed the gates, we suddenly heard a noise coming from behind the walls of the graveyard. "Thump Thump.............Thump Thump............Thump Thump!"

As the noise got louder, I grew more scared and wondered what could be making the noise. "Thump Thump...............Thump Thump...................Thump Thump!"

However, Pepper was not as curious as I was. Once she heard the noise, she immediately took off running back to our rectory. Although she is supposed to be my protection, she wasn't going to be around to see from what I was going to need to be protected!
"Thump Thump......................Thump Thump........................Thump Thump!"

Once she took off running, I took off running, too.
"Thump Thump......................Thump Thump........................Thump Thump!"

When I look behind us, would believe that I saw a coffin coming out of the cemetery and heading towards us. It was standing on it's edge moving in our direction. "Thump Thump...................Thump Thump...............Thump Thump!"

The quicker we ran, the quicker the coffin began to follow us.
"Thump Thump...........Thump Thump............Thump Thump!"

Once we made it to the rectory, we ran inside and locked the doors.
"Thump Thump....Thump Thump....Thump Thump!"

And, the coffin smashed right through the wooden door.
"Thump Thump....Thump Thump!

So, we ran up the stairs.....
        And the coffin followed us.
                "Thump Thump!"

We ran into my bed room.....
> And the coffin followed us.
>> "Thump Thump!"

We ran into the bathroom....
> And the coffin followed us.
>> "Thump Thump!"

So, I opened the medicine cabinet,
> hoping to find something to throw at the coffin.
But all I could find was a bottle of Robitussin.
> "Thump Thump!"

So, in horror, I tossed the bottle at the coffin......
> "Thump!"

And, would you believe
> (just hold ya' breath for this one)

The Coffin Stopped!

Because.....Robitussin can always stop a "Coffin Attack!"[54]


When I look through Sacred Scripture, I assure you that there are several episodes that would not have been recorded if I were one of the Four Evangelists. We are all lucky that the quartet of Matthew, Mark , Luke and John were not dependant on Tony recording any of the events in the life of Jesus.

If they were waiting for me to help write the scriptures, we would have never been able to read about the raising of the Widow's Son in the City of Nain[55], the raising of Jairus' Daughter[56] or the raising of his friend Lazarus[57].

---

[54]It's OK to laugh out loud! Don't act like you didn't see that one coming!

[55]Luke 7:11-17

[56]Matthew 9:18-26; Mark 5:21-43; Luke 8:40-56

[57]John 11:1-44

Because, if I see just a blade of grass move by somebody's grave, I'm not going to be there to find out what else is going to happen!

So, first we ought to thank God that the four Evangelists either saw for themselves or had wonderful sources that recorded these blessed events for themselves. In knowing that Jesus can raise the dead, we know that he can bring us through anything that we face.

In the raising of Lazarus, for example, we experience the power of Christ at one of the greatest peaks.

> When Mary, the sister of Lazarus, came where Jesus was and saw Him, she knelt at His feet and said to Him, "Lord, if you had been here, my brother would not have died." When Jesus saw her weeping, and the Jews who came with her also weeping, He was greatly disturbed in spirit and deeply moved. He said, "Where have you laid him?" They said to Him, "Lord, come and see." Jesus began to weep. So the Jews said, "See how he loved him!" But some of them said, "Could not he who opened the eyes of the blind man have kept this man from dying?"
>
> Then Jesus, again greatly disturbed, came to the tomb. It was a cave, and a stone was lying against it. Jesus said, "Take away the stone." Martha, the sister of the dead man, said to Him, "Lord, already there is a stench because he has been dead four days." Jesus said to her, "Did I not tell you that if you believed, you would see the glory of God?" So they took away the stone.
>
> And Jesus looked upward and said, "Father, I thank You for having heard Me. I knew that You always hear Me, but I have said this for the sake of the crowd standing here, so that they may believe that You sent me." When He had said this, He cried with a loud voice, "Lazarus, come out!"
>
> The dead man came out, his hands and feet bound with strips of cloth, and his face wrapped in a cloth. Jesus said to them, "Unbind him, and let him go." Many of the Jews therefore, who had come with Mary and had seen what Jesus did, believed in Him.[58]

---

[58]John 11:32-45

In this story, that comes from the Eleventh Chapter of the Gospel of our Brother John, we hear a story that has many different meanings and messages. Throughout it, we experience the many facets of Jesus' ministry, and the many ways we have come to know and love the Lord.

In retelling this life-giving story, we meet the Jesus of Love and Compassion, we meet the Jesus of Healing, and we meet the Jesus of Reconciliation and Forgiveness.

Through the story of Lazarus, we meet the Jesus that has come to call each of us out of our deadly tombs of Temptation and Sin and into the Born-Again world of Salvation.

My Brothers and Sisters, as we know from this gospel account, Lazarus was a very close friend of Jesus. So, when Jesus heard that His friend, Lazarus, was dying, he traveled from Jerusalem to Bethany to be with Lazarus' sisters, Mary and Martha, and to bring about a miracle that would bring many doubters to believe that He truly is the Son of God.

When He arrived in Bethany, Mary and Martha both greeted Him with the same statement: *"Lord if you had been there, my brother would never have died."* Jesus told both of them that their brother was not dead. For, indeed, he will rise again. He, then, asked them to take Him to Lazarus' Tomb.

At the tomb, Jesus instructed them to roll away the stone that was blocking the entrance to the grave. Now, you could only imagine the reactions of the people around them.

Lazarus had been dead for four days before Jesus even got to Bethany. Therefore, his body would have begun to decay. *"Lord, by now, there will be a stench."* Martha said. Let's just say that the smell inside the tomb was not going to be pleasant. But, Jesus insisted that the stone be rolled away.

When they did, Jesus looked up to heaven, gave thanks to God and called out with a loud and clear voice, *"Lazarus, come out!"*

At the command of Jesus, the Bread of Eternal Life, the dead man came out of the tomb. St. John tells us that as he came out his hands and his feet were still tied with the *traditional, Jewish,* burial bands. Seeing that Lazarus was now free from death, Jesus looked at the people and said, *"Untie him and let him go!"*

People of God, in a very real way, we are all like Lazarus. There are many aspects of our lives which lead us into the dark and damp tombs of temptation and sin.

Within these tombs, we find endless sickness, heart ache, and grief. Ultimately, our tombs can lead us away from life and to eternal death.

Just pause for a moment and look at world around us. Look at the many things that tempt us to turn our backs on God and on our fellow human beings. There are many things that lead or tempt each of us to fall into the traps of sin.

The hard part about these sinful temptations, these tombs of temptation, is that the things that really tempt us usually feel good. In fact, if it didn't feel good, it wouldn't really be tempting. That is why it is so difficult to resist temptation.

But like Lazarus, we have a choice. We can either cross the thresholds of our tombs of temptation and sin or we can remain among the dead in these tombs.

Part of our problem is that some of us have become so comfortable in our tombs that it has become difficult to hear the voice of Jesus calling us out. We have actually convinced ourselves that this is the way that it is supposed to be!

In fact, some of us have been in the tomb so long that we have fixed it up, and made it so comfortable, that we don't want to leave.

In our tombs of sin, we have gotten comfortable sitting on our stolen furniture, watching our illegal cable television and eating our scrumptious meals that were bought with a fake food stamp cards! And, yet we wonder why nothing around us seems to be coming to life. It is because we have chosen to make our homes among the dead!

Each of us deals with the deadly elements of temptation and sin on a daily basis. No one is immune to being tempted. Even Jesus, during His 40-day retreat in the desert, was tempted by the Devil. The key is you don't have to bow to temptation.

God, the Father of Mercy and Love, sent Jesus Christ to call each of us forth from our tombs, just as He called Lazarus. Through the Death and Resurrection of Christ, we have been saved from the sinfulness of humankind. However, to receive the full benefits of our salvation, we must respond to God's call. We must be willing to leave behind our tombs.

That is why Jesus Christ is standing at the door of our tombs and yelling to each of us, "Come Out!"

Each day, we must remember this call to salvation and eternal life. Once you respond to Christ's call, you then have a new role in helping to bring about the salvation of others. Remember in the Gospel, when Lazarus came out of the tomb, his hands and his feet were bound. Seeing this Jesus told the crowd to "Untie him and set him free."

The image that we have is of Lazarus, calmly walking out of the tomb. But, if I was in the tomb and I heard Jesus calling me, I would have been jumping out of that tomb, hand and feet still bound!

Those who already know the loving forgiveness of Jesus Christ are called to be the "untie-ers," the ones who do the untying. Once you have come to know and love Jesus, our Lord, you must be willing to bring others to that level of love.

Many people carry with them burdens from long ago. These burdens are the cloth burial strips that tie our hands and feet.

For some, it may be a sin that you have already confessed but can't bring yourself to a point of self-forgiveness. For others, you may have hurt someone but haven't been able to seek their forgiveness. While for others, you may have been hurt by someone else and have not been able to truly forgive them as God forgives you.

These are some of the burial bands that those who are called to salvation can bring with them. But, I assure you that you can't get across the doorway of Life, past the Gates of Heaven, if you are still bound with these burial bands.

Others are called to help untie those who are trapped in these bands. The Sacrament of Reconciliation or Penance is one of the ways that our Church can help to untie you and let you go free.

Unfortunately, not enough people are willing to take advantage of this Sacrament of Untying, the sacrament of release and freedom.

The Sacrament of Penance is a visible sign that you have stepped out of your tomb of Temptation and Sin.

Our God is truly a good God.
Our God is truly a loving and forgiving God.

As we know, nothing is impossible with God on your side.
No stone is too big for God to roll away.
No tomb is too old for God to call you out of.
No band is too tight for God, His people and the Church to untie.

All you need to do is Trust in God!
All you need to do is COME OUT OF THE TOMB!

Jesus Christ is standing at the door of our tombs and yelling to each of us, "Come Out!"

I have come to know my Jesus as "the Resurrection and the Life."

I have come to hear my Jesus call me out of the Tombs of Temptation and Sin.

I have heard His cry and exited the tomb.

Can you hear Him?

Today, may the God of Forgiveness and Grace call you out of your tombs of sin and temptation, untie your burial bands of sin and finally, yes finally, let you go free.

You know as good as Robitussin can be at stopping a coughing attack, only the Love of Jesus can stop a real coffin attack!

So, in the name of Jesus, don't let the tomb or the coffin catch you!

---

*Wealth is useless on the day of wrath,*

*but virtue saves from death.*

Proverbs 11:4

# To Err is Human

How do I forgive you when I know that you hurt me on purpose?
How do I continue to look you in the eye when I know that you haven't stopped trying to hurt me?
How do I live with the knowledge that even though I never intentionally tried hurt you, you did everything in your power to hurt, defame and destroy my life?
How do I forgive you when I know you hurt me on purpose?

My brothers and sisters, one of the harshest realities of life is the fact that we hurt one another and we often do it on purpose. We do it with our words. We do it with our deeds. We do it with our bad intentions and our pretentious desires. We hurt one another and we often do it on purpose.

In facing this harsh reality, we are also faced with an even tougher position: How do I forgive you when I know you hurt me on purpose?

I once heard that "to err is human and to forgive divine." I wonder if that means that I don't have to forgive people since I'm not divine but forgiveness is? If forgiveness is divine, maybe only God has to forgive people for their sins. But, "to err is human." So, even if I don't have to forgive, I have to at least realize that I am human and I will err. I will do something that is wrong and I will do it on purpose.

So, what's so divine about forgiveness?
What makes the act of forgiving so holy?

First, we must realize that true forgiveness comes directly from God. Time and time again, our Heavenly Father has had to *"forgive us our trespasses."*[59] Quite often, God has had to touch our very souls and wipe away our sins.

When we sinned against God and His church, He forgave us.
When we broke one of His Commandments, He forgave us.
When we hurt Him by hurting one of His earthly sons or daughters,
He forgave us.

God has forgiven us far more times than we have ever deserved. That is why "to err is human." That is part of the reality of our lives. "But, to forgive is divine." That is part of the reality of our God.

---

[59]See Matthew 6:12 and Luke 11:4

68

But, we must be keenly aware that in forgiving us of our trespasses, God turns to us and calls us to then "forgive those who trespass against us."

Forgive those who trespass against us - knowingly or unknowingly.
Forgive those who hurt us - on purpose or unintentionally.

*"Forgive those who trespass against us."* In doing this, we do for others what God has repeatedly done for us. But, we should also be aware that the act of forgiveness is not an act of just giving to others. It is also an act of freeing one's self.

I once read,

> The act of "Forgiveness is the miracle of a new beginning.
> It is to start where we are, not where we wish we were,
> or the other person was. It is to hold out a hand; to want to
> renew a friendship; to want a new relationship with husband,
> father, son, daughter, friend, or indeed my enemy.
>
> It may not take away the hurt. It does not deny the past injury.
> It does not ignore the possibility and need for repentance and
> a change in the relationship. It means being willing to take
> the initiative in dealing with any barriers that I may be raising
> towards a restored relationship.
>
> It means that I am willing to have a relationship with the other
> party that is based on Christian love and not on what has
> happened in the past, if the response of the other person makes
> that possible." [60]

In other words, I must strive to forgive those who have hurt me, not just for their sake, but really for my own sake. In offering forgiveness to another person, I really am offering freedom to myself. Letting go of the hatred in my heart makes room in my heart for the blessings of God!

Another reality of forgiveness is the fact that no one can make me forgive a person who has hurt me. Forgiveness is part of the internal forum. It is part of the mind, heart and spirit. Thus, I must chose to forgive someone. It can't be forced.

---

[60] http://www.christianity.co.nz/forgive3.htm

I remember back in the old days, when I was in elementary school. Whenever we had a fight on the school yard, the teachers would make you stand up in front of the person you were fighting and say, "I'm sorry." And after, the other person said, "I'm sorry," too, you then shook hands as a sign of forgiveness. But, more times than not, as you were looking each other in the eyes, you were not offering forgiveness, you were probably saying, "3:00 PM at the Oak Tree, let's finish this!"

Even though it looked like forgiveness was being offered, reconciliation was not actually taking place.

Today, God calls us to be men and women of true forgiveness - not just because it will be an act of letting go and letting God be the judge but because it is an act of freeing oneself.

The Father in the parable of the Prodigal Son[61] forgave his child. God, our Father, forgives us. Who, then, are you called to forgive?

*"To err is human but to forgive divine."* To err is to bind up yourself and others. To forgive is to set yourself and others free.

Today, through the Grace of God, may you finally be able to let go of the past hurts of your life. May God give you the strength to loosen the bounds of your heart and allow self-healing to begin. May you see the err of your unforgiving ways, and work now to be the loving person that God has called you to be.

Today, In the name of Jesus, our Suffering Servant, may God forgive you as you forgive those who trespass against you.

How do I forgive you when I know you hurt me on purpose?

I look to the cross and realize that He forgave me, even though He knew that I put Him there on purpose. Today, is the day to forgive.

Lord, *"forgive us our trespasses as we forgive those who trespass against us."*

Amen.

---

[61]Luke 15:11-32

# The Dog and the Lie Competition

The other day, I was walking down the street and I saw a bunch of boys, all standing around this cute little dog.

Every time that I looked at them, they would all would start to giggle.

So, I walked up to them and said, "Gentlemen, I know that you are not about to try and hurt that dog."

And, one little boy replied, "Oh no, Father, we love the dog. And we decided that *whoever could tell the biggest lie* could have the dog."

One little boy raised his hand and said, "Well, my Daddy is Shaquille O'Neil. And, he flies home every Sunday to play basketball with me." And, all the kids replied, "nah...nah....nah....."

So, another lil' boy said, "Well, my Daddy is Barack Obama! And, I can go anywhere in the country that I want to....." And, all the kids replied, "nah...nah....nah....."

So, another lil' boy said, "Well, my Daddy is Bill Clinton!" (*"Well, anything is possible.....*) And, all the kids replied, "nah...nah....nah....."

So, I said, "Gentlemen! Don't you know that lying is a sin. It says it right there in the Bible, *"Thou Shalt Not bear false witness against thy neighbor."*[62] That means that we ain't supposed to lie. "In fact, when I was your age, I never told a lie."

To which a little boy, replied, "Alright, give him the dog."

And Jesus said,

> *"For although you have hidden these things from the wise and the learned you have revealed them to the childlike."*[63]

---

[62]Exodus 20:16

[63]Matthew 11:25

How often have we come across children whom seem to be too wise for their age? Now, I am not talking about children who think that they are "grown!" That's a whole 'nother thing. I am talking about children who are truly wise. So wise, that you wonder if they have been here on Earth before.

I think that part of their wisdom comes from being able to see life without having experienced the disappointments and struggles that can come with truly being "grown." They haven't yet had to deal with the day to day headaches and heartaches that can come with being adults or trying to raise a family in this materialistic and sometimes heartless world.

They are able to see life for what it truly is, a gift from God that is to be lived and lived to the fullest.

If only we, the adults, could learn from the wisdom of our little ones. For, "Although *God has* hidden these things from the wise and the learned *He has* revealed them to the childlike."[64]

The Wisdom of God's Love is all around us. But, we cannot really experience it unless we see and hear God's Words from the perspective of a child.

That's why the Prophet Zechariah stresses that no matter what happens in life, We ought to rejoice.

Rejoice because soon and very soon, our King shall come to rescue us from all of the trials and tribulations of this life. And, when He comes, everyone will get their just rewards. Those who have been faithful to God will join Him in His reign and dominion over the Earth. Those who have not been faithful will find themselves banished from Jerusalem, banished from the New Jerusalem, which is the Kingdom of Heaven.[65]

In child-like wisdom, it really is that simple.

St. Paul in his Letter to the Romans, reminds us that in child-like wisdom, we must live according to the Will of God, according to the Spirit that dwells inside of us.

---

[64]Matthew 11:25

[65]See Zechariah 9:9-10

If we live according to the flesh, meaning if we allow the desires of this world to control our lives, we will never be able to enjoy life as God intended for His children to enjoy. Living according to the flesh means getting all caught up in the traps of this world.

Ya'll know what that is all about:
It's when obtaining material goods become more important than serving God.

It's when sexual desires and physical gratification becomes more important than truly loving God and caring for your neighbors.

It's when becoming number one at work or school becomes more important than spending time with your family and those who love you.

Living according to the flesh means that the values of this world begins to supersede the values that God and your family have taught you.

St. Paul assures us that if you *"live according to the flesh, you will die."*[66] And, that death may not be just a physical death, but, life as you know it will also die. Jesus said, *"For, you cannot serve God and mammon."*[67]

Simply put, either the God of Abraham, Isaac and Jacob will be your God or the Ways of this World will be your god. Only one can get you into Heaven. It's up to you to decide which way you will be headed!

On many occasions, Jesus tells us that our lives as adults should be as simple as our lives were as children. For, as little ones, God reveals to us, what He has continually revealed to His children throughout all generations.

A simple (child-like) revelation is the fact that the only way we can come to now God the Father is through Jesus, His Son. Just as a child comes to know about God through the loving words and caring deeds of his or her parents. We come to know God the Father through the loving words and the spirit-filled deeds of Jesus, our Savior.[68]

---

[66]Romans 8:13

[67]Matthew 6:24

[68]See Matthew 11:27

Another child-like revelation is the fact that we as adults can find true rest only when we turn to God and ask for it. We know this because Jesus has said to us,

> *"Come to Me, all you who labor and are burdened, and I will give you rest. Take My yoke upon you and learn from Me, for I am meek and humble of heart; and you will find rest for your selves. For My yoke is easy, and My burden light."*[69]

At the end of the day, a child knows that the most comfortable and secure place on Earth is in the loving arms of his mother or father.

At evening time, a child falls asleep in the arms of his or her parents, simply because in their parents' arms they feel that nothing on this Earth can harm them.

Children of God, in our Heavenly Father's arms, we find that same peace that a Child finds in his or her parents' arms. Wrapped in God's arms, we can truly find rest.

Another child-like revelation can be understood as Jesus says, *"Take My yoke upon you and learn from Me. . . For, My yoke is easy and My burden light."*[70]

In hearing this with the ears of adults, and interpreting this passage with adult-like wisdom, we know that part of the message is the fact that God will never gives us more than we can handle. For, *"His yoke is easy, and His burden is light."*

But, if you listen to this revelation with child-like wisdom, you may also get another message. For, in the simple understanding of a child, you may come to realize that Jesus said, *"take My yoke upon you."*

He did not say, "take My harness upon you or be harnessed with My burdens." That is a key element in this passage.

For, a harness is what you put on a horse or a mule in order for that animal to pull a plow or a wagon. But, do you know that a yoke is not a harness? A yoke is an apparatus that is put on the necks of a pair of animals, almost like a double harness so that together they can pull the heavy plow or wagon.

---

[69]Matthew 11:28

[70]Matthew 11:28

In other words, with a child-like level of revelation, When Jesus said, *"take My yoke upon you and learn from Me,"* He was saying, "With My yoke, together We can pull all the burdens that life places on your shoulders. For, with My yoke, you will be harnessed on one side and I will be harnessed with you on the other side. Thus, together, nothing in this world, no struggles of the adult life, no burdens of the flesh, no troubles on your jobs could ever wear you down."

For, with Jesus helping you to pull through whatever the Father allows to come upon your shoulders, you not only will make it, but, like a child, at the end of the day, you will find rest, a peace full rest in the Protective Arms of God, the Father.

My brothers and sisters, sometimes when life becomes so burdensome that we can't figure out what to do, we ought to turn and look at life through the eyes of a child. For Jesus said, *"Although you have hidden these things from the wise and the learned you have revealed them to the childlike."*[71]

If only, when we get "grown," we could still see through the eyes of a child. Then, we could truly live life as God intended it to be lived.

On this day, may God give you the strength to be as courageous as an adult, but as wise as the child.

---

*He who seeks the good commands favor,*

*but he who pursues evil will have evil befall him.*

Proverbs 11:27

---

[71]Matthew 11:25

# Mea Culpa, Mea Culpa

Over the past ten years or so, an expression has crept into our common language that tries to sum up our attitude toward human failings. Back in the old days, when someone made a mistake or did something that they knew was wrong, they would usually say, "I'm sorry" or "Pardon me." But, now, in this modern time, instead of saying "I'm sorry," many simply say, *"My Bad."*

At first, when you hear some one simply say, *"My Bad,"* it may sound as if they are attempting to dismiss their mistake with a simple statement or even deny responsibility.

But, the fact is, saying, *"My Bad,"* is almost a literal translation of a Latin phrase that used to be part of our penitential rite. Remember, back in the dinosaur days, when you would say, *"mea culpa, mea culpa, mea maxima culpa."* You were saying, "My fault, my fault, my most grievous fault." Or simply put, *"Oh Lord, My Bad."*

Despite being a fairly recent phenomenon, this little exclamation may be very close to the spiritual truth. In a time when we try to write off our own mistakes and failings, we can still face the fact that we are wrongdoers. We can still be trapped by the lure of Sin.

There are an awful lot of people in this world who need to be standing before the Altar and saying to God, *"My Bad."*

In fact, if we took a few minutes to do so, everyone of us could come up with a list of the top ten people we consider sinners, the people we feel have broken the laws of God and made our world a worse place. Depending on our race, ethnic cultural or political views, our lists might vary to some extent but I think we can all agree that we know sinning when we see it.

And so, if we allow ourselves to do so, we can indeed point out the big sinners of our day. I'd bet that if we look around our churches, today, we can select a good bunch of sinners, right there in House of God.

But, before we start writing down the names of all the sinners we can see in our churches, we had better make sure that we put our own name right there at the top of the list. Because, if we're honest with ourselves and with God, we have to agree that we are sinners, too.

Each one of us has done, and continues to do, things we're not so proud of. Thus, as we stand before our God, instead of judging and condemning others, we had better be saying, *"mea culpa, mea culpa, mea máxima culpa"* Or more simply put, *"Oh, Lord, My Bad."*

You see, if we really want to see sin removed from the world, we have to start by recognizing and acknowledging our own faults and failings. Only then will we be able to allow God to forgive and heal us and thus heal our sinful world.

Throughout Sacred Scripture, we can see that our God is a loving and merciful God. All He really wants from us is that we acknowledge that we are sinners and turn our hearts to Him. But, even in His mercy, God expects us to seek out His forgiveness.

For example, in Chapter 6 of the Book of the Prophet Hosea, Hosea tells us of God's efforts at reconciliation with Israel. In this chapter, the prophet tells us that God's coming is like the dawning sun and spring rain. But, in this dawn of God's love, unfaithful people (sinners) are like morning clouds and evaporating dew.

Hosea used this imagery to point out that God is not pleased by false piety and mere words of conversion. *"It is love that I desire, says the Lord, not sacrifice."*[72]

In other words, what God wants from us is genuine love and devotion and not fake Christians who go to Church because it makes them look good.

God wants true examples of faith. He wants true followers. That's why in his Letter to the Romans, St. Paul uses the story of Abraham and Sarah to inspire the Christian community. The lives of these great ancestors inspire us to remain faithful even when the obstacles we face in this sinful world seem insurmountable.

It was Father Abraham's faith and hope that made it possible for him to fulfill his destiny as the Father of a great nation. Despite the fact that he was almost 100 years old, and Sarah wasn't far behind, God had promised Abraham that if he remained faithful to his calling, he and Sarah would have more descendants than they could ever count. Even though he didn't know how that would be possible, Abraham was confident that God would carry out His promise.

---

[72]Hosea 6:6

*Abraham did not doubt God's promise in unbelief; rather, he was empowered by faith and gave glory to God and was fully convinced that what he had promised he was also able to do.*

*That is why "it was credited to him as righteousness."*

*But it was not for him alone that it was written that "it was credited to him";*

*it was also for us, to whom it will be credited, who believe in the one who raised Jesus our Lord from the dead, who was handed over for our transgressions and was raised for our justification.*[73]

In this story, St. Paul compares belief in the Risen Christ to the illogical faith of Abraham and Sarah. If God could produce a Nation of People from an old man and a barren woman, surely, He could save the world, through the Death and Resurrection of Jesus Christ. And, in that Resurrection, He could offer forgiveness to the world.

In the Gospel from the works of our Brother Matthew, Jesus makes it clear that He came to call sinners. He did not come to call the self-righteous. Despite the critics who complained about His spending time with tax collectors and sinners, Jesus made it clear that He came to bring forgiveness to all who seek God with a sincere heart.[74]

Back in Jesus' day, the Jews despised tax collectors because many of the tax collectors often took advantage of taxpayers. But, Jesus called the tax collector Matthew away from his old life. He called him to see that his life was not all that God had to offer. By eating dinner with Matthew, other tax collectors and sinners, Jesus vividly showed the world exactly who He came to serve.

In His actions, He sent a message to the self-righteous people of His day that simply pointed back to the words of Hosea, *"It is love that I desire, says the Lord, not sacrifice."*[75]

---

[73]Romans 4:20-25

[74]See Matthew 9:9-13

[75]Hosea 6:6

When He heard the Jews complaining about His association with known sinners, He responded saying, *"Those who are well do not need a physician, but the sick do."*[76] Jesus went on to say, *"I desire mercy, not sacrifice. I did not come to call the righteous but sinners."*[77]

When we bring these words into our modern times, we can all go back to that Top Ten list of folks that we could create of all the sinners in our world, in our Church and in our families. We could definitely begin to write down the names of people that we have already condemned to Hell, "In the name of Jesus." But, in doing so, we become no better than the self-righteous people of Jesus' day. We become no better than the very same people that Jesus shamed in the Gospels.

If we are truly His followers we must realize that we are called not to reject sinners but, to actually to spend time with the marginalized and outcasts in our world.

How can they believe in a Christ whom they have never seen or heard?

How can they encounter Christ, if they never meet Him in His followers?

Christ calls us to do as He did, to reach out to those we label as "sinners."

By being judgmental and exclusive Christians, we actually reject those whom Jesus wants us to embrace. That is why I fully believe that our own healing and forgiveness depends on our ability to extend God's love to others, especially those whose sinfulness has hurt us or hurt those we love.

Throughout history, Jesus has continued to reach out to those who are in need of God's healing and forgiveness. As the followers of Christ and believers in His Gospel, we are called to do as He does and be agents of healing and forgiveness.

But, in order to do so, we have to first admit that we, too, are sinners and are in constant need of His love and forgiveness. Just as only the sick need doctors, only repentant sinners need a Savior.

Thus, if you cannot acknowledge that you are a sinner, you really have no need for Christ Jesus, our Lord and Savior.

---

[76]Matthew 9:12

[77]Matthew 9:13

That is why we pray,

I confess to almighty God,
and to you, my brothers and sisters,
that I have sinned through my own fault,
in my thoughts and in my words,
in what I have done, and in what I have failed to do;
and I ask blessed Mary, ever virgin,
all the angels and saints,
and you, my brothers and sisters,
to pray for me to the Lord our God.

May Almighty God have mercy on us,
forgive us OUR sins and bring us to everlasting life.
Amen.

Today, before the Throne of Grace, we say,
*"mea culpa, mea culpa, mea maxima culpa."*

"My fault, my fault, my most grievous fault."

Or simply put, *"Oh Lord, My Bad."*

---

*A single reprimand does more for*

*a person of intelligence*

*than a hundred lashes for a fool.*

Proverbs 17:10

# Jesus, My Spiritual GPS

As many of you know, I entered Notre Dame Seminary in 1990. Back then, I walked away from a successful time as a public school teacher and decided to give my life, my love and even my legacy to God.

Little did I know then, what God would be doing with me now. Back in 1990, I never could have imagined all that I would be doing today to spread the Word of God. From pastoring one of the best parishes in the Archdiocese of New Orleans to traveling the world preaching the Good News, indeed, God has blessed me with a wonderful life, simply because I was willing to enter the seminary and turn my life over to Him.

Since 1990, I have been blessed to teach and preach in almost every part of the United States of America, and as a result of those great opportunities, I have become one of the most sought after speakers on the national circuit.

Almost daily, I get invitations to give revivals, to speak at conferences or to lead seminars for teachers and preachers. Every day, I am fielding emails from across the country asking if I would be available to visit their region. I get so many invitations, that I can only accept about one fourth of them.

Do you know that I am already booking revivals for the next two to three years? That's how much folks are dying to get me to visit them.

When folks invite me to come and speak to them, I always laugh when they begin the negotiation process. I usually get the "it must be expensive to get you" kind of stuff. For some reason, folks around the country believe that it must cost a lot to get me to come and speak at their place. (And, I don't blame them. If you want the best, you've got to pay the best!)

But, they are always shocked when they ask, "How much does it cost to get you?", and I reply that I really don't have any set fees or set amounts for what I do. The day that I have "set prices" will be the day when this life becomes my job and not my vocation. When it comes down to stipends and gifts, I leave it up to God.

But, since I have become a *prima donna* preacher, I have developed a list of things that I ask for when I travel. You know, the kind of stuff that celebrities require when they are booked for an event. The stuff that folks must supply before a presenter will commit to an event.

And, so, when invited to speak somewhere, these are the logistics that I request:

1. I only fly Delta Airlines. I like Frequent Flyer Miles and now that I have reached the highest level in the program, I almost always get free upgrades to First Class.

2. A hotel room needs to be provided. I do not like to stay in church rectories because I really like to get away and be by myself.

3. A rental car should be provided, depending on how long my stay will be. I love to get out and see the place.

4. I require four ziplock bags of M & M's all separated by color. I only like the green, red, brown and yellow ones. All other colors need to be discarded and possibly burned with the palms for Ash Wednesday Services. The new colors are certainly inferior to the original colors!

OK, the M & M's thing is negotiable!

Believe it or not, most places will go out of their way to meet these four requests. And, who would blame them! I'd do the same things to get me, too!

Of all the things that I ask for, the one thing that they often question me about is the request for a rental car. Most speakers prefer to be picked up by someone and chauffeured around the region while they are there. I've been to places where they've sent a limo to get me or they have a person assigned to pick me up. But, I really prefer to drive myself.

I like the freedom of coming and going whenever I choose.  But, I guess that their fear is that I may get lost trying to find the places where I will be preaching. So, they want to send somebody to make sure that I get where I need to go and make sure that I am in the right place at the right time.

Little do they know, when I travel, I always bring somebody with me who knows exactly how to get to the various speaking engagements. You see, I have a GPS system that will get me to wherever I need to be. All I need is an address and my little Global Positioning System and I am good to go!

It doesn't matter where I am in the United States or Canada, my GPS will guide me, turn by turn, directly to where God needs me to be. There's nothing like having a system that works to make sure that you don't get lost along your way.

When I am traveling along, I am listening to a sweet voice saying, "Left turn, 500 yards," "Exit ahead" and "You have reached your destination." There is nothing like the comfort and confidence that I have in that sweet little voice that is telling me where to go and how to get there. I love my GPS.

As Christians, we too have a GPS to help us get to our final destinations. In all four of the Gospels, Jesus lets us know that He will always be with us to lead us in the right direction.

In the Gospel of John,

> Jesus said to His disciples, "Do not let your hearts be troubled. You have faith in God; have faith also in Me.
>
> In My Father's house there are many dwelling places. If it were not, would I have told you that I go to prepare a place for you? And if I go and prepare a place for you, I will come back again and will take you to Myself, so that where I am you may be also. Where I am going you know the way."
>
> Thomas said to Him, "Master, we do not know where you are going. How can we know the way?"
>
> Jesus said to him, "I am the Way, and the Truth, and the Life. No one comes to the Father except through me."[78]

In this passage, Jesus tells His disciples that although He was about to leave them, He was headed to Heaven get the place ready for their arrival. He was headed to prepare their rooms in the Mansion of His Father. And, then once the rooms were ready, He was coming back to get them.

Although He was planning to come back and lead them to the Mansion, he assured them that they already knew how to get there.

When St. Thomas, spoke up to say, *"Master, we do not know where you are going; how can we know the way?,"* Thomas was basically saying, "Lord you are about to leave us and we really don't know where you are going and what we are supposed to do until you come back."

---

[78]John 14:1-6

83

And that is why Jesus responded to his question by saying, *"I am the Way and the Truth and the Life."* In other words, "Thomas and the rest of ya'll, just follow my lead, and I will give you life in great abundance."

*"I am the Way, and the Truth, and the Life.*
*No one comes to the Father except through me."*

People of God, in this deep and profound statement, Jesus Christ summed up all that we need to know about life and true happiness. In this statement, Jesus put in simple but yet profound words, all that we need to understand if we truly want find happiness both in Heaven and right here on Earth. In this deep statement, Jesus sums up for us, the very reason why He endured the incarnation and crucifixion. He did is so that He could show us the way to the Father.

*"I am the Way, and the Truth, and the Life.*
*No one comes to the Father except through me."*

In being *"the Way,"* Jesus is in a very modern way, the GPS system for which we have all been longing. In being *"the Way,"* Jesus has mapped out for us a pathway that leads directly to the Kingdom of Heaven.

For 40 years, Moses and the Hebrew Children wandered in the desert trying to find their way to the Promised Land. If only they had a GPS, they would not have had to wander, they could have taken a direct path. If only they knew the Way!

For years, mankind has search the earth for the pathway to happiness. We've followed many man-made maps, only to get lost and end up hopeless and in despair. If only we had a GPS to show us where we could find our little pieces of Heaven right here on Earth.

Even now, folks are still trying to find their way out of depression, heartache and disappointment. If only we had a GPS system that could step in and illuminate and exit right out of the darkness of despair.

Well, in a very real way, Jesus who is *"the Way,"* is the GPS system that we need.

Jesus could have made Moses' route a lot simpler. Because as we know, Jesus shows is the pathway to happiness here on Earth. It is Jesus and only Jesus that can truly guide us out of the darkness of despair. Indeed, Jesus is the illuminated tracking system that promises to lead us and guide us along the way.

84

But, a major part of having Jesus as our GPS, is being able to accept Jesus, who is *"the Way,"* as also being *"the Truth."*

You cannot truly follow the Way of Christ, if you are not willing to live in the Truth that is Christ. Living in the Truth that is Christ means that you may have to accept some of the disappointing elements of life as being a part of that Truth.

Some of those truths are Happiness is found inside of your heart and soul in relationship with Jesus who is the Way. This means that you will never be able to find true happiness if you are searching for it in this world or in other people. True peace comes from within.

The world, as part of it's nature, is a dying thing. It will not last forever. Eventually, even the greatest things of this world will one day crumble. But, the Kingdom of Heaven is eternal. It will never end. Thus, true happiness is not found in all the things we have here. True happiness will be permanent in the World that is to come.

Living in the Truth means that we sometimes have to face the pains and disappointments that not only things of this world but also the people of this world will bring into our lives.

It is hard for children to accept the fact that "our parents are not perfect." They often make mistakes. But, we are called to listen to them when they speak the Truth because God has chosen them to help us find our way to Jesus.

It is hard for parents to accept the fact that our children are not perfect. They like us, are sinners by nature. This means that they can fall into the traps of sin. Part of the problems that our society is facing today are due to the sinful nature of our children. But, I would hold that one thing that is compounding those problems is the fact that many parents are not willing to face the Truth and believe that their children are capable of such great sins.

We could solve many of our heartaches if we are willing to accept the fact that those once little innocent angels can indeed be caught by the ways of this world and fall into lifestyles that are not of God. It is time for parents to face the Truth and realize that no child, no teen, no person is above the temptations of sin.

The Truth of the matter is, we are all sinners in need of salvation.

So, neither you or your child are perfect.

Parents, if your child is wrong, then he or she is wrong! To hold them as righteous, even when you know the Truth, is as sinful as the criminal and immoral acts that they might be committing. That is part of "the Truth" that is Jesus.

Jesus says, to us, *"I am the Way, and the Truth, and the Life."* And, sometimes, the Truth hurts!

If you follow Jesus who is *the Way*, And you live in Jesus, who is *the Truth*, you can indeed find the pathway to happiness and the pathway to eternal life.

The life of joy that Jesus promises us is not just some transparent thing that can only be achieved when we get to Heaven. It is not some transitory thing that will only be experienced in spurts here on Earth. It is a life of true happiness that begins here on Earth and is truly fulfilled when we cross over the threshold of the Mansion that Jesus is preparing for us in the Kingdom of His Father.

If you truly follow *the Way* of Christ, you can find true happiness right here on Earth. But, you have to live in and accept *the Truth*.

Today, God calls all of us to examine our lives and compare them to the pathway that he has cut which leads directly to the Kingdom of Heaven.

Are we living according to the ways of Christ or are we living according to the ways of the world, the ways of sin?

Do we live in *the Truth* or are we living lives of lies that are systematically eroding away the joy that Christ promised us?

Simply put, are we truly followers of Jesus or are we living a lie?

*"I am the Way, and the Truth, and the Life."*

He couldn't have put it any simpler.

*"I am the Way, and the Truth, and the Life."*

He didn't say, "I am one of the ways or I am part of the truth or I am some of the life." He said, *"I am THE WAY, and THE TRUTH, and THE LIFE."*

That means that if you follow Him, and live according to His Word, in the end, you are going to be alright.

You know, when I travel around the country, folks worry that I just might get lost along the way. But, I have deep trust in my little GPS system to get me wherever I need to be.

But, as much as I trust my GPS system, it can't come close to how much I trust my Lord to lead me and guide me along the way. Oh, that GPS voice that tells me, "left turn 300 yards," or "exit ahead then take the highway," is really nice to have. But it will never come close to the voice in my heart that say, *"Do not let your hearts be troubled. You have faith in God; have faith also in me."*

It can't compare to that voice in my heart that says, *"No one comes to the Father except through me."*

It can't be compared to that voice that says, *"I am the Way, and the Truth, and the Life."*

People of God, a GPS system can get us to almost any place on Earth. But, only Jesus can get us to our rightful places in the Kingdom of Heaven.

Today, it is my fervent prayer that you will allow Jesus to lead your along the pathways of life so that you can truly enjoy the happiness that comes from living in the truth and nothing but the truth.

Because, when you live in the truth, Jesus who is *THE TRUTH* lives in you.

---

*He who loves correction loves knowledge,*

*but he who hates reproof is stupid.*

Proverbs 12:1

# Protect the Children: From Womb to Tomb

Since May 27, 1995, I have been having a good time being a Roman Catholic Priest for the Archdiocese of New Orleans. In this role, I have had the opportunity to speak to many churches and gatherings (literally) around the world.

I have celebrated the Sacraments in almost every part of the Continental U.S. (North, South, East and West). I have anointed the sick in Los Angeles, celebrated the Eucharist on the shores of the Sea of Galilee and even rededicated people during a Baptism-like celebration in the River Jordan.

I have heard confessions in people's homes. I have celebrated the Rite of Confirmation as we welcomed a new parish member into full Communion with the Church, and I have presided at numerous weddings in my Archdiocese.

The only Sacrament that I have not had the opportunity to preside at is the ordination of a deacon or priests. You have to be a bishop to ordain someone.

God has surely blessed me with many great opportunities: opportunities to proclaim His loving commitment to His Chosen People through the liturgical life of the Church.

All of our Sacraments are filled with God's Blessings. Our Church comes alive when the people of God gathers to hear His Words and experience his compassion through liturgical celebrations.

Though I enjoy presiding for and celebrating all of the Sacraments, there is one of the Big Seven that I really enjoy celebrating. That is the Sacrament of Baptism. How blessed we are to welcome new members into our fold as they welcome the Holy Spirit into their lives. I particularly enjoy celebrating the baptism of a new baby.

There is something about the baptisms of new babies that lets us know that God is still moving and working in our lives. God knows that without babies continually coming into the Church, the Church would eventually grow old and literally die. Thus, new babies mean new life for a faith community.

Not only does the presence of the babies bring a message to us from God, but also the presence of the adults at the Baptismal Celebration. The presence of parents, families and God-Parents at baptisms lets us know that people are willing to take the responsibility of assuring the Church that the child will grow up knowing God through the Faith Practices of the Roman Catholic Church.

Baptisms also give adults an opportunity to renew not only their Baptismal Promises but also their commitment to sharing their faith through practicing it in a Roman Catholic Church.

One of the most popular scripture passages read at Baptisms is taken from the Gospel of Mark. In the Tenth Chapter of Mark we hear:

> *And people were bringing children to Him that He might touch them, but the disciples rebuked them. When Jesus saw this He became indignant and said to them, "Let the children come to Me; do not hinder them, for the kingdom of God belongs to such as these. Amen, I say to you, whoever does not accept the kingdom of God like a child will not enter it." Then He embraced them and blessed them, placing His hands on them.*[79]

In this passage, Jesus takes children in His arms, embraces them and blesses them. This is truly one of the most tender moments in Sacred Scripture. It shows the depth of God's concern for His little ones: His out-stretched arms, His loving embrace and His offering of love. What more could we ask?

In reading this passage, we can be so taken by this loving image that we can sometimes miss the stern warning that God gives the adults as a major part of this passage.

Jesus says, *"Let the children come to Me; and do not hinder them."*

Sometimes people are so caught in the loving scene of Jesus welcoming the children that they miss the *"do not hinder them part."*

When I think about the plight of the unborn children in our nation, we know that there are many ways that adults can hinder children from growing up with a clear and sincere knowledge of God.

---

[79]Mark 10:13-16

One way we as a society have hindered our children is through the legalization of abortions. How much more hindrance can there be than the willful removal of a developing baby from its mother's womb?

The baby growing inside of a mother's womb cannot defend itself from predators. It is at the mercy of the mother dependant on her for nourishment and protection. To not protect the child is to hinder him or her from growing up knowing that God is God and that all human beings are His people.

Another way we can hinder them is by rearing them in homes where love that was once sacramentally-professed on the Altar of God is shattered by the sins of a mother or a father. Children, who experience divorce, experience the break down of a sacramental covenant. Sometimes they can be the forgotten victims of their fighting parents. They, too, are victims of the divorce and can be hindered from gaining a true knowledge of God whose covenant with us is unending and unbreakable.

Still another way that we hinder our children from coming to God is by allowing our society to pass laws which are contrary to the teachings of our faith. Any law which does not protect the dignity of the individual, the sanctity of marriage and the lives of those who cannot protect themselves is a law against the Laws of God.

Children who grow up in communities which do not protect a person's basic right to life are hindered from full knowledge of their inherent dignity and the love of the Creator who calls us to uphold that dignity.

People of God, as I travel around the globe proclaiming the Good News, I really do have a good time. Through the Grace of God, I have written and delivered some very powerful sermons in the Name of Christ Jesus.

I may even tell a good joke or two.

But, when it comes to the protection of life, *from Womb to Tomb*, I never joke.

There is nothing funny about the willful neglect or taking of a human life. There is nothing funny about the willful neglect or disregard for a person's inherent dignity as a Child of God. There is nothing funny about the harm that millions of children, born and unborn, face each and every day.

I may joke about a lot of things, but I will never joke about the willful destruction or harming of a Child of God.

Better for you to be hurt, defiled or defamed than to be *thrown into the fires of Gehenna* because you chose to hinder a child's sacred movement toward God.

My Family in Christ,
Today, I want you to sincerely ask yourself,
have I in anyway hindered a child from coming to Jesus?

Have I hindered their knowledge of God through my words or deeds?

Have I hindered a child from experiencing the dignity that is rightfully given to them by our Creator?

Have I hindered a Child of God, young our old, a child, physically able or disabled, a child, intelligent or mentally challenged, a child of my race or of another race, have I hindered a child of God in anyway as they tried to get to Jesus?

And if I have in any way, shape or form, hindered a child's path to Jesus, what must I now do to atone for my sins?

Jesus says, *"Let the children come to me; do not hinder them, for the kingdom of God belongs to such as these."*[80]

Better for you to be hurt, defiled or defamed than to be *thrown into the fires of Gehenna* because you chose to hinder a child's sacred movement toward God.

If you have hindered or are hindering a child, My fervent prayer for you is May God have mercy on your soul.

---

*If a son ceases to hear instruction,*

*he wanders from words of knowledge.*

Proverbs 19:27

---

[80]Mark 10:14

# The Devil Made Me Do It

Back in the early 1970's, Comedian Flip Wilson was on top of the television market with his variety comedy show. Long before there was a Dave Chapelle or an Eddie Murphy, Flip Wilson was commanding the market as one of the funniest men on television.

On his variety show, he featured many special guests like Dean Martin, Redd Foxx, Paul McCartney, Gina Lollabrigida, and Muhhamad Ali. The "Flip Wilson Show" debuted in 1970, and was an instant hit.

Flip's comedy was the real focal point of the series. In various skits, he played a collection of regular characters, which included: The Reverend LeRoy of the *"Church of What's Happening Now,"* a gospel preacher who seemed to be slightly less than honest but was a pretty good fundraiser, Danny Danger, private detective, and Herbie, the Good Time Ice Cream Man, are just a few of the characters he played as parts of his act.

Of all of Flip Wilson's characters, the one that most folks remember was the glorious Miss Geraldine Jones. Now, just to jog your memory, Geraldine was Flip's female persona. To play her Flip would wear a blond wig, an extremely short skirt, and pair of high heels.

Geraldine was not the prettiest woman you could imagine. And, that's a good thing. Geraldine was a sassy, swinging, liberated woman with a very jealous boyfriend named "Killer." Even though we never ever saw "Killer," she kept telling folks that he was coming there.

Through his character, Geraldine, Flip Wilson has been credited with creating some of the biggest catch phrases in television history. Geraldine was the first to get on TV and say, *"When you're hot, you're hot; when you're not, you're not."*

Now, her most famous line is what came to my mind when I was thinking about this reflection, because every time, Miss Geraldine Jones found herself getting into trouble, she would look up and say, *"The Devil Made Me Do It."* Lord, who could ever forget, Geraldine and her very memorable line, *"The Devil Made Me Do It."*

You know, when I was a young child, I was really afraid of the Devil. From the way folks acted and the way some folks talked, the Devil seemed to always have the power to control everything.

When something went wrong in your life, it was because of the Devil. When you said a bad word, it was the Devil in you talking. When you committed a sin or did something that you knew was wrong, some how it was the Devil that made you do it.

You know, as a young child, growing up and hearing all this stuff that the Devil could control and make you do, I couldn't help but be afraid of the Devil.

What if the Devil tried to control me like he was apparently controlling others? What if the Devil visited my house and made everybody do what he commanded? What if the Devil took over not just my house but my family, my city, the world? The Devil must be a mighty powerful being if he could do all that folks claimed he could do.

Throughout Sacred Scripture, we hear about men and women who remained committed to the Will of God, even though it seem as if the Devil was trying to turn them away from the Lord. Time and time again, the great men and women of the Bible show us how the power of God will continually defeat the power of the Devil.

In the Book of Jeremiah, Chapter 20, the Prophet speaks as if the Devil himself was talking through him. He says to God,
> *"You duped me, O LORD, and I let myself be duped; You were too strong for me, and You triumphed. All the day I am an object of laughter; everyone mocks me."*[81]

Now, this can also be translated as, "You seduced me, Lord, and because I allowed myself to be seduced by you, people are making fun of me." Here, Jeremiah is saying that because he decided to follow God, to be His messenger, the world seems to be against him.

But, Jeremiah shows that the Love of God is far more powerful than the Devil when he says,
> *"I say to myself, I will not mention him, I will speak in his name no more. But then it becomes like fire burning in my heart, imprisoned in my bones; I grow weary holding it in, I cannot endure it."*[82]

---

[81]Jeremiah 20:7

[82]Jeremiah 20:9

In other words, knowing about God's Grace and Mercy is too much for him to hold in. He's got to proclaim it. Because when he doesn't proclaim God's Word, it becomes like a fire burning inside.

St. Paul also felt the internal pull between Good and Evil that Jeremiah spoke of in his book. In the 7th Chapter of Paul's Letter to the Romans, he speaks about how internally he knows what he is supposed to be doing, yet more often than not, he does what he's not supposed to do.

In this great letter, St. Paul says,
> *"For I do not do the good I want, but I do the evil I do not want. Now if (I) do what I do not want, it is no longer I who do it, but sin that dwells in me. So, then, I discover the principle that when I want to do right, evil is at hand."*[83]

That is why in Chapter 12 of this very same letter, Paul says to us,
> *"I urge you therefore, brothers, by the mercies of God, to offer your bodies as a living sacrifice, holy and pleasing to God, your spiritual worship."*[84]

In this, he is say to us, "Don't allow the ways of the world to become your God. Do what is good, be renewed in the Spirit and thus, you'll be pleasing in the eyes of the Lord." This means that we must be on guard to make sure that the Devil doesn't take control of our lives. We must take control of the Devil and let God lead the way. We can only do this if we work towards having a transformation of our hearts from hearts that listen to and are afraid of the Devil to hearts that focus only on the Love and the Will of God.

Even Jesus Christ had to be on guard against the powers of the Devil. In the 16th Chapter of the Gospel of Matthew, Jesus shows us how to deal with the Devil when The Prince of Evil tries to get in our way. In Verse 21, Jesus tells the disciples about the path God has chosen for Him to be glorified. He says,

> *"He must go to Jerusalem and suffer greatly from the elders, the chief priests, and the scribes, and be killed and on the third day be raised."*[85]

---

[83]Romans 7:19-21

[84]Romans 12:1

[85]Matthew 16:21

Now, when Peter heard this, he pulled Jesus aside, and said, *"God forbid, Lord! No such thing shall ever happen to You."*[86] In other words, "Jesus, don't let it end this way. It will be a disgrace to You and the Father and to us!"

In his "always say the wrong thing at the wrong time" way, Simon Peter shows us how the Devil can try to block the path of God, as God tries to communicate His Loving Plan to His Chosen People.

Jesus immediately recognized Peter's caution for what it was. It was the Devil speaking! And so Jesus responded with *"Get thee behind me, Satan."*[87]

Now, I don't think that Jesus thought that His best friend, Simon Peter, was actually the Devil. But, Jesus knew that it was something evil speaking in Peter that needed to immediately be rebuked. When Jesus said, *"Get thee behind me, Satan,"* He was saying, "I know the Will of God, I accept the Will of God, and I refuse to let you or anything else stop Me from doing the Will of God."

Children of God, when I was younger, I was truly afraid of the Devil. If the Devil was something or some kind of force that could cause folks to do the wrong thing, or say the wrong thing or even think the wrong thing, then I really needed to be afraid.

You see, when you analyze it, fear can be a good thing.

When you are afraid of something, you recoil back from the thing you fear and avoid going near it. If only others could be as afraid of the Devil as I was, what a better world this would be. For, rather than entering into a relationship with the personification of Evil, they would recoil or draw back from the very Force of Evil that causes mankind to do wrong.

You know, I have to admit that even today, I am still afraid of the Devil.

Oh, now don't get me wrong, I am not scared of some mythical horned-fellow with a pitch fork and a red face. No, I ain't scared of that Devil.

What I am afraid of is the great power of evil, the real Devil, that forces folks to do what they know they ought not do, that forces folks to fall, time and time again, into the traps of temptation and sin.

---

[86]Matthew 16:22

[87]Matthew 16:23

See that's the Devil that I am afraid of.

We, as God's Chosen People, ought to start rebuking that Devil just as Jesus rebuked Satan when he tried to impede the path to God's Glory.

You see, if more folks walked around saying, *"Get thee behind me, Satan,"* rather than saying, "The Devil made me do it," what a better world this would be.

We ought to look at those things that lead us into committing the Seven Capital Sins, the deadly Forces of Evil and say, *"Get thee behind me."*

To things that lead to Pride, the deadly sin which makes us want to be exalted above others and even above God, to the Sin of Pride, we ought to say, *"Get thee behind me."*

To things that lead to Gluttony, the sin that places a priority on physical satisfaction and mental gratification, rather than on the virtues of restraint and temperance, to the Sin of Gluttony, we ought to say, *"Get thee behind me."*

To things that lead us to Avarice or Greed, the sin that makes us want more than we really need, to the Sin of Greed, we ought to say, *"Get thee behind me."*

To things that lead us to Lust, the sin that makes us see other human beings as objects for our sexual gratification, objects of sexual indulgence, to the Sin of Lust, we ought to say, *"Get thee behind me."*

To things that lead us to Sloth, the sin that is best translated as just-plain-Laziness, you know, the temptation to do nothing constructive, to the Sin of Sloth, we ought to say, *"Get thee behind me."*

To things that lead us to Envy, the green-eyed sin that causes us to resent the good things other people have received or achieved. The sin that causes us to see the ability of other people, their talents, gifts, diligence, and energy as reasons to dislike both the person and their achievements. To things that lead us to the deadly Sin of Envy, we ought to say, *"Get thee behind me."*

And finally, to things that lead us to the Sin of Anger, the sin through which we encounter an expression or a feeling of resentment toward someone else. To the Sin of Anger, we ought to say, *"Get thee behind me."*

My brothers and sisters, to anything that leads us into the deadly sins of Pride, Gluttony, Greed, Lust, Sloth, Envy or Anger[88], we ought to say, *"Get Thee Behind Me."*

I fully believe that through the waters of Baptism, God's Holy Spirit moved in and took up dwelling in my soul. And, it is from my soul and through God's Spirit that I now have the power to control all things and the people that might tempt me to stray off the path that God has chosen for me.

There is no power within us or around us that is more powerful than the Love and Providence of Our God. Thus, to say, the Devil made you do, you've got to lie. To say, it was the Devil talking, you've got to lie. For, if you have been Baptized, if you have accepted Jesus Christ as your personal Lord and Savior, if you have come to know and feel the love of God in your lives, then you can't keep blaming your sins on this mythical character known as the Devil.

You have to take control of yourself, and know that with God's Spirit within you, nothing will be able to defeat your desire to do God's Will.

On this day, let us firmly say,
"Get thee behind me, Satan, 'cause I am going to see my Lord."
"Get thee behind me, Satan, 'cause I know that the Lord is Good."
"Get thee behind me, Satan, 'cause I know my Redeemer lives."

"Satan get your hands off me."
"Satan get your hands off my child."
"Satan get your hands off my world."

'Cause, I belong to the Lord and it was from thee that Jesus set me free!"

Today let us proclaim to the Power of Evil that our God, who dwells with us, is more powerful than anything thing that can come at us from the outside.

Today, let us look at the evil temptations of this world, and say,
*"Get Thee Behind Me, Satan."*

---

[88]For more on the Seven Capital Sins see Bishop Donald Wuerl's article, *"Our Catholic Faith: The Seven Capital Sins,"* Columbia Magazine, August, 1999, The official Magazine of the Knights of Columbus.

# YouTube of Faith

By now, most of the world has heard of YouTube. But, for the folks that don't know what it is, YouTube is the latest computer fad that allows almost anyone to upload videos to the internet so that they can be viewed by almost anyone around the world.

If you log on to YouTube.com, you can see videos of police chases, old television shows and folks fighting in the streets of America. Some people even upload their personal home videos. That means that you can see videos of Pookie's lil' baby dancing in the streets. You can see pictures of somebody's Uncle Harry falling off of a ladder. You can even see videos of a lady with a belt teaching her teenage son a solid lesson on why you should never talk back to your momma.

By logging on to YouTube, you can see almost anything. Even politicians have come to learn about YouTube. Many of them are uploading their speeches and videos from various public appearances onto the website in hopes of attracting the votes of the younger generation.

President Barack Obama has credited YouTube and other video sources like it for helping to promote his agenda to the youth. What the fireside chats on the radio used to be for President Franklin D. Roosevelt, uploads to YouTube have become the venue for the 44th President of the United States.

Now, President Obama and other politicians are not the only folks that are now using YouTube to get their messages out. Even Churches are now using YouTube. If you do a quick search using words like Catholic, Homily, Altar Server, and Catholic Gospel Choir you can find videos of some wonderful Church related stuff. Of course, you also have to weed through a bunch of junk that are just jokes or parodies about our church and our faith.

In fact, I didn't realize my celebrity status until I put my own name in the YouTube search engine and found a video of me saying Mass in Los Angeles, speaking at the National Catholic Youth Conference, and laughing with the youth in the Diocese of Honolulu.[89]

---

[89]In the search engine at www.YouTube.com, type "Father Tony" and prepare yourself to be amazed.

It is amazing how quickly stuff will appear on YouTube. If a politician or athlete or religious leader does anything of note (good or bad), by the time the sun goes down, you can bet that somebody uploaded a video of it on YouTube.

When I look at the life of our Church and all of the marvelous events that took place in our history, I was thinking about YouTube. What a blessing it would have been if somebody back then could have shot videos of the big events and then uploaded them to the internet for the world to see. I especially wish that we had videos from the major events in the life of Jesus Christ. Those videos would definitely be the most viewed videos on the world wide web. Unfortunately, there were no video cameras back then. The closest that we can get to being there is through reading and listening to the accounts of the Apostles. Let us thank God for the Gospels, the Acts of the Apostles and the letters that St. Paul and other holy men wrote to their communities.

Scripture is great, but in these modern times, we can all agree that a video would help us even more. If YouTube was up and running back in the time of Jesus, St. Joseph could have uploaded movies from that first Christmas. Mary could have uploaded videos from Jesus' Childhood years, his first Passover Meal, his first day at Hebrew School, and even his first time riding on a donkey. We could also have videos of the stuff that the Apostles experienced. We could download videos of Jesus healing the lame, walking on water and even feeding the multitudes.

A Bible Times version of YouTube definitely would help a lot of us get a better understanding of all that took place back when Jesus walked the Earth. When we read the accounts of the Resurrection appearances, for example, wouldn't it be nice if the Disciples had had a video camera and a computer with them in the Upper Room on that first Easter Night. Although there was no YouTube for us to vividly see everything back then, we are tempted to read the accounts of the Resurrection, as if they were videos from the past, vivid photographic descriptions.

> *On the evening of that first day of the week, when the doors were locked, where the disciples were, for fear of the Jews, Jesus came and stood in their midst and said to them, "Peace be with you." When He had said this, He showed them His hands and His side. The disciples rejoiced when they saw the Lord.*[90]

---

[90]John 20:19-20

What a blessing it would be if we could actually see Jesus coming through that locked door, showing Himself to His friends. We could better share in the rejoicing of the disciples, if we had a video of that blessed moment. Yet, how much greater your experience of faith can be when you don't have a picture or video to prove what you believe in?

For the disciples, the Resurrection was a vivid experience of faith. Their faith experiences with the Risen Lord was so strong that they dared to do what He did. All of the Resurrection accounts show us people who came to believe very strongly that Jesus was risen from the dead. Once they believed, they were willing to do something about it. They went out and told their friends. Although they did not have a video to show folks, they still went out and told the world. But, a video of that first appearance would have helped.

We can see, as we read and reflect on those first Resurrection accounts that there were some people in Sacred Scripture that had a hard time believing that Jesus was risen. We can see that the news of the Resurrection that was first brought by the women was dismissed as hysteria. Some of the Apostles thought that the girls were crazy for believing that they had actually seen angels and heard angelic messages of the Lord's rising. Other Scripture Stories tell us of how Jesus reprimanded some of the post-Resurrection witnesses for their lack of faith. Later in John 20, we hear about the greatest time of doubt, as we listen to the story about the Great Apostolic Doubter, *Thomas*. A video would have definitely helped Thomas.

> *Thomas, called Didymus, one of the Twelve, was not with them when Jesus came. So the other disciples said to him, "We have seen the Lord." But he said to them, "Unless I see the mark of the nails in His hands and put my finger into the nail marks and put my hand into His side, I will not believe." Now a week later His disciples were again inside and Thomas was with them. Jesus came, although the doors were locked, and stood in their midst and said, "Peace be with you." Then He said to Thomas, "Put your finger here and see My hands, and bring your hand and put it into My side, and do not be unbelieving, but believe." Thomas answered and said to Him, "My Lord and my God!" Jesus said to him, "Have you come to believe because you have seen Me? Blessed are those who have not seen and have believed."* [91]

---

[91] John 20:24-29

In this passage, we can see that although many in that Upper Room probably harbored doubts about all that was being reported, only Thomas had the courage to voices his doubts.

Thomas basically said, "Unless I see Him and I touch Him, *I'm not going to believe.*"

One week after making such a statement, Thomas did see and touch the Risen Lord. His doubts turned to solid faith. His statements of little faith turned into one of the greatest professions of faith, *"My Lord and My God."*

Through writing the Acts of the Apostles, St. Luke continued writing about the events in the lives of the Apostles after their Resurrection experiences. The Acts of the Apostles speaks of many signs and wonders worked in the Name of Jesus by the Apostles.

> *Many signs and wonders were done among the people at the hands of the apostles. They were all together in Solomon's portico. None of the others dared to join them, but the people esteemed them. Yet more than ever, believers in the Lord, great numbers of men and women, were added to them. Thus they even carried the sick out into the streets and laid them on cots and mats so that when Peter came by, at least his shadow might fall on one or another of them. A large number of people from the towns in the vicinity of Jerusalem also gathered, bringing the sick and those disturbed by unclean spirits, and they were all cured.*[92]

Like Jesus did before them, the Apostles went about doing good deeds in the Name of Jesus: healing the sick, proclaiming the Word and taking care of the poor. Even Peter's shadow had healing properties.

Man, how great it would have been to have a video of St. Peter's shadow passing over somebody being healed.

What we can take from these written accounts is the fact that as the Apostles acted in faith, more and more believers were added to the Lord. In a very real way, the Apostles' faith became contagious. It spread throughout the land.

---

[92] Acts 5:12-16

When you think about it, Old Doubting Thomas shows us what it was that the witnesses to the Resurrection believed. Thomas asked to see the wounds of Jesus. The Risen Lord in whom he would believe was the crucified Jesus, who had suffered and died on a tree.

If that Jesus could show up alive, then God was indeed faithful to the Word who became Flesh, emptying Himself to take on the nature of a slave, becoming obedient even to death. The death of Jesus became for Thomas and the other disciples, what the Gospel of John says it is, a true Passover to the Father.

Jesus, as a human being, risked everything. He gambled that the Father would not let Him down, and He won. Jesus had faith in the Resurrection, long before His Crucifixion!

His Faith called Him to do the Father's Will!
His Faith called Him to shun this World for the Glory that was to come!
His Faith called Him to action!

Well, like Jesus, our Resurrection faith is a faith that calls us to action, too.

When Jesus appeared in the Upper Room to the Disciples, the Bible tells us that He breathed forth the Holy Spirit. It is that Spirit that enables the believer to continue the work of Jesus. In the *Acts of the Apostles*, St. Luke tells us that the apostles dared to imitate the actions of Jesus.

They forgave sins.
They proclaimed the Good News.
They celebrated the Lord's Supper.

Because they believed, they took the risk of acting in the Spirit.

They gambled and won.
They understood then, just as we should understand now that wherever He goes, Jesus, the Risen Lord, brings His Spirit of Peace.

The disciples in the Upper Room were far from peace.
They were sad that Jesus had died.
They were frightened that what happened to Him would happen to them.
They were huddled in uncertainty and disappointment.

In coming to them, the Risen Lord dispelled all their pain and fear. And, because of this, "*the disciples rejoiced when they saw of the Risen Lord.*"

The Lord, in the Book of Revelation says, *"Do not be afraid. I am the first and the last, the one who lives. Once I was dead, but now I am alive forever and ever."*[93]

People of God, as follower of God, we are called to put our faith in the Risen Lord Jesus. We are called to believe, even though we do not see. We are called to face the sorrows, the disappointments, the pains of life and to keep believing.

We are also called to bring our confidence in the Risen Lord to the world outside of the upper rooms where we are tempted to huddle and hide.

We are invited to bear witness to life when we face death, to bear witness to peace when we see war, and to bear witness to joy when we know sorrow.

If we believe: miracles will happen. If we believe: many will be healed and forgiven, many will be added to the Lord. If we believe: we will never die, but have everlasting life.

You know, I am, so glad that we really don't need YouTube or any other video source to help us believe in the Resurrection of the Lord. All we need is the Sacramental Life of our Church and the power of the Holy Spirit.

For, in the Spirit, with eyes of faith, we can truly see God!

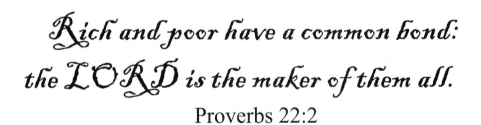

*Rich and poor have a common bond: the LORD is the maker of them all.*
Proverbs 22:2

---

[93]Revelation 1:17-18

# SECTION THREE
## Lessons from Fr. Tony

# Rev. R. Tony Ricard, M.Th., M.Div.
## *St. Augustine High School*
## *Class of 1982*

# Standing at the Crossroads:
# The Four Moments of the Sun

*The Ordinary Passages of Life* are amply defined by author Robert Farris Thompson. In his book, *Flash of the Spirit: African and Afro-American Art and Philosophy*, Thompson describes these passages through using "The Four Moments of the Sun" or the Kongo Cosmogram. Thompson writes that all primary elements of life can be compared to the circular movements of the sun. Thus, the circle is one of our most sacred symbols in life.

To the Bakongo People (West Africans), all of human existence is a continuous motion on the Circle of Life. The Rising and Setting of the Sun are used to signify the Birth and Death of human beings (The Rising and Setting of Human Life). The periods in between birth and death are marked by the stages of earthly maturation. Of these earthly maturation periods, the Moment of the Elders receives the highest esteem.[94]

This holistic view of life teaches that the existence of any given community must be seen through the whole. Existence is not found in the particular. The Ancestors, the Elders, the Adult Community, the Child and those Yet-To-Be-Born have special movements in the collective Dance of Mankind.

*All persons at The Sacred Transitions of the Sun*
*must see themselves as distinct representations of the whole.*

The First Moment of the Sun contains human life from birth to childhood. The Second Moment moves us from childhood through adolescence. The Third Moment takes us from our youth through our adulthood. The Fourth Moment moves us from adulthood through the period of the Elders. Our earthly journeys are completed when we move from the Fourth Moment into the Spiritual World, the World of our Ancestors.

By connecting this aspect with our Catholic Faith, we can see that the ideals of the Four Moments of the Sun have consistently been included in our faith traditions and rites.

---

[94]Robert Farris Thompson, *Flash of the Spirit: African and Afro-American Art and Philosophy,* (New York: Vintage Books, 1983), pp. 103-159.

This "African-American Stuff" ain't nothing new to the Catholics. For Catholics, our journey from conception through being Born-Again to reaching the age of reason is achieved in the First Moment of the Sun. The Second Moment takes us from our confirmed full-membership in the community through our ordained or vowed covenants with God and each other. The Third Moment of the Sun moves us from these adult covenants through our roles as Elders, and ordained and lay leaders in the community. Our path as ordained and lay Elders into our time of purification by God occurs in the Fourth Moment. We faithfully believe that our course is completed when we pass on to eternal life with our Creator.

Regardless of our spiritual positions in the Four Moments, we are all worthy of God's Love. *African-American Spirituality consistently stresses that no Moment of the Sun is deemed in and of itself to be better than the whole.*

Our individual dignity is not found in the particular but rather in the communal. We become a truly Catholic Church when everyone in the Four Moments is recognized and made present to the Circle of Christ: The True Circle of Life!

Traditionally, we refer to this common dignity and interconnected Catholic-Circle of Life when we profess our belief in the *Communion of Saints*. We believe that all are connected through the love of Jesus Christ. In Him, the Church is a communion of holy people *(sancti)*.

In the *Credo of the People of God: Solemn Profession of Faith*, Pope Paul VI expounds on this by writing, "We believe in the communion of all the faithful of Christ, those who are pilgrims on Earth, the dead who are being purified, and the blessed in Heaven, all together forming one Church."[95]

Each person has a specific movement that is needed for the collective Dance of Creation. But, with our movements in this collective dance, there comes responsibility. In particular, those who have entered the Period of the Elders must seize the reigns of the community.

Through their connectedness with the Ancestors, many of whom are rightfully called the "Elders of the Elders", they must lead and guide the people of God. It is their collective charge to shepherd the Sheep of the Creator.

---

[95]*Apostolic Letter of the Supreme Pontiff Paul VI: Credo of the People of God*, paragraph 30

The Bakongo People and most West African communities have always taught that Authentic Elders are fully embodied with *Áshe*.[96] Deep within each of them is the power to make things happen. *Áshe* makes them beacons of "God's enabling light rendered accessible to men and women."[97] One who has fully commanded the powers of *Áshe* is rightfully admitted to the Sacred Council of Elders.[98]

Now, don't think that the concept of *Áshe* is something new or foreign to the Catholic Faith. All I have to do is ask you, "What is Grace?" and I am sure that you will be able to connect *Áshe* with our Faith Traditions.

*Áshe is the Wisdom-Filled Grace of God.* Thus, those who possess *Áshe* are fully aware of the indwelling of the Holy Spirit which comes through our Baptisms.

Now, the term Elder does not automatically mean that one is chronologically old. Just as the passage of years does not automatically make one an Elder. My Grandmother used to say, "Old age don't make you wise. It only makes you old."

Only the wisdom-filled possession of *Áshe* can allow one into the Moment of the Elders. Some young people have assumed the roles of Elders because of their Divine Gift of Wisdom. The Prophet Jeremiah is a prime example of a chronologically-young Elder. Though he was young, he was given the gifts of Prophetic Wisdom.[99] It was through the grace of God that Jeremiah and all Elders became beacons of the Ancestors to the people in their midst.

Even as we reflect on the Elders, *what must be stressed is that no particular Moment of the Sun is deemed in itself better than the whole.* For, all exist for the sake of the whole. All are responsible for the life of the whole. *"No one has made it, until all have made it."* Thus, we all are called to hold on to each other, making sure that the *"circle will be unbroken."*

---

[96]*Áshe* has also been spelled *axe* in some cultures of African Descendants (especially in Brazil).

[97]Thompson, p. 5.

[98]No one can obtain *Áshe* through their own merits. It is sent through the spiritual world of the ancestors by the Divinity. In possession of *Áshe* one is given the fully-functional gift of wisdom. One, consequently, enters into the Elders' Moment of the Sun.

[99]See, *The Call of Jeremiah (Jeremiah 1:4-11).*

As a people, we must proclaim that when any person is missing from the circle, the collective plan for salvation is not being fulfilled.

In Jesus, we are called to invite all peoples to active participation in the dance. Unfortunately, as a Church, we have not consistently sent out this invitation.

Thus, the questions before us this day is, how can we learn to better invite our brothers and sisters to the Banquet Table?

As Church, we are a primary part of the Creator's Dance which is the Circle of Life. We are collectively responsible for assuring our God that the dance will happen according to His Will.

If any Members of the Circle are not present, we are compelled to call them back to the dance. We must be true dancing evangelists. Together, we, the Church will bring the dance to its climax at God's Altar in Heaven. But, for now, we are sending out an invitation to the entire Catholic Community to come to the teaching circle and learn how to dance. That we all might delight in being truly Catholic and truly Free.

*"And before I'd be a slave, I'd be buried in my grave
And go home to my Lord and be free."*[100]

===

*The glory of young men is their strength,
and the dignity of old men is gray hair.*
Proverbs 20:29

---

[100]*African-American Spiritual*

# We're Going to the Super Bowl!

Once there was a football fan sitting in the top row at the Super Bowl. Although he was excited to be at the National Football League's annual championship game, he was a bit disappointed because he could barely see the field from his lofty seats.

As he glanced through his binoculars, he noticed that there was a vacant seat on Row 3, only a few feet from the field. Not only was this seat on the third row. It was also directly in the center of the stadium, on the Fifty Yard Line.

Throughout the First Quarter, this very choice seat remained empty. As the Second Quarter began, he decided to go down and see if anyone had arrived to claim the seat. As he approached the seat, he noticed an older gentleman sitting in the adjacent seat. So, he asked him if anyone was sitting there.

The gentleman replied by saying, "No, son, so come on in and have a seat."

After a few minutes of watching the game from this wonderful vantage point, the young man turned to the older gentleman and said, "This is one of the best seats in the house. I can't figure out why it would be empty. How is possible that someone could buy a ticket for the biggest sports event of the year and then not use the ticket?  Do you know to whom this seat belongs?"

"Of course, I do," he replied. "You see, my wife and I have been fans of our team for more than 40 years. Every year we promised one another that if our team ever made it to the Super Bowl that we would be there. After our team was victorious in the playoffs, we bought our two seats. But, unfortunately, last week my wife passed away."

Feeling a bit sad, the young man asked, "You didn't have a son or daughter or even a friend that could have come to the game with you?"

To which the gentleman replied,  "No........They're all at the funeral."

People of God, to real NFL fans, football is more than just a game. It's a way of life. It's a cultural experience. From the beginning of Training Camp to the last play of the Pro Bowl, everything we say and do revolves around our team's football schedule and all of the news and sports programs that discuss the game. Football is indeed a way of life!

For true fans, Super Bowl Sunday is a day that surpasses even Thanksgiving Day when it comes down to having millions of people glued to couches and recliners, watching the NFL on TV.

On Super Bowl Sunday, a day on which New Orleans Saints Fans traditionally repeat the phrase, "Wait till next year," football will be on many people's minds.

Rather than giving you a long exegesis on the existential ramification of people who are caught in the misdirected paradigms of an avaricious society, I have decided to write a reflection on the wealth of terminology used during football games.

In a very real way, football terminology can apply directly to our experiences in Church. For much of what takes place on Sundays, on the gridiron of a football field, also takes place on Sundays on the Battlefield of the Lord.

Here are a few Football Terms.

### Blocking:
On the football field, Blockers are very large men who position themselves in front of the defenders in order to prevent them from getting to the Quarterback.

In Church, Blockers are the folks who at the end of Mass position themselves in front of the Pastor and talk endlessly thus preventing others from getting to him!

### Draft Choice:
On the football field, a Draft Choice is a person who has been picked to play for a specific team during the annual NFL Draft.

In Church, a Draft Choice is what happens when that Little Old Lady wearing a sweater comes into Church and begins looking for the air conditioning vents before she chooses her seat.

### End Zone:
On the football field, the End Zone is the part of the field where touchdowns are scored.

In Church, the End Zone are the particular pews where the priest's homily topics actually make sense.

### Extra Point:
On the football field, an Extra Point is what you get if you kick the ball between the goal posts after a touchdown has been scored.

In Church, an Extra Point is what you get when you tell the young associate that his sermon was too long.

### Illegal Motion:
On the football field, an Illegal Motion is when an offensive player is penalized for moving before the play has officially started.

In Church, Illegal Motion is when you should be penalized for leaving Church before the final blessing.

### Defensive Interference:
On the football field, Defensive Interference is when the defender hits the offensive wide receiver before the football arrives.

In Church, Defensive Interference is when the priest begins to tell the Church about an up-coming change in the way we do things and you start shaking your head "no" before you let him finish.

### Two-Minute Warning:
On the football field, the Two-Minute Warning is when the referee blows his whistle and alerts both teams that there are only two minutes left in the half or in the game.

In Church, the Two-Minute Warning is when that Little Old Lady in the front row starts looking at her watch to signal the preacher that his sermon has gone too long and that she will only be awake for about two more minutes.

### Quarterback Sneak:
And, finally, on the football field, the Quarterback Sneak is when the Quarterback runs the football through the center of his blockers rather than handing it off to the Running Back, like everyone expects him to do.

In Church, the Quarterback Sneak is when you receive The Holy Eucharist and head straight for the exits thinking that no one (including God) sees you leaving Church early.

Who would have thought that football terminology and church activities can go hand in hand?

I guess that it takes the minister interpreting the words for us.

People of God, on Super Bowl Sunday, we are surrounded by so many things and words from the world of Football and the television commercials that go with this big game, that we can become isolated from what is really essential.

We can lose sight of what it really means to be happy or blessed.

Over the span of the last 20 years, companies have spent over 1.84 Billion Dollars for 30-seconds commercials to promote their product during the big game.

With all of the "pre-game hype" on Super Bowl Sunday, many folks can get so caught up in the football game and rooting for their favorite team that they run the risk of becoming lost. They can somehow lose sight of the really essential aspects of our existence.

Chapter 5 of the Gospel of our Brother Matthew calls us to be cautious on days like Super Bowl Sunday so that we may not lose sight of the real world.

We must stay in touch with God and remember our core foundations and the reasons why we were created "In the beginning....."

We are called to be loyal to God and not just to our favorite football team. And more importantly, we are called to reaffirm our relationship with Jesus Christ through recognizing our connectedness with others.

In "The Sermon on the Mount," Jesus shares with us the *Beatitudes* or as my old scripture from the seminary, Fr. Frank Montalbano, OMI, would say, the "Be-Attitudes: The Attitudes of Being."

> *When Jesus saw the crowds, He went up the mountain; and after*
> *He sat down, His disciples came to Him.*
> *Then He began to speak, and taught them, saying:*
> *"Blessed are the poor in spirit,*
> *for theirs is the kingdom of heaven.*
> *Blessed are those who mourn,*
> *for they will be comforted.*
> *Blessed are the meek,*
> *for they will inherit the earth.*
> *Blessed are those who hunger and thirst for righteousness,*
> *for they will be satisfied.*

*Blessed are the merciful,*
*for they will be shown mercy.*
*Blessed are the clean of heart,*
*for they will see God.*
*Blessed are the peacemakers,*
*for they will be called children of God.*
*Blessed are those who are persecuted*
*        for the sake of righteousness,*
*for theirs is the kingdom of heaven.*
*Blessed are you when they insult you and persecute you and*
*utter every kind of slander against you falsely because of me.*
*Rejoice and be glad, for your reward will be great in heaven."*

And, anyone who is a fan of the New Orleans Saints knows what it means to be Poor in Spirit & Humble of Heart. Saints Fans know what it means to mourn and to be persecuted.

In this powerful sermon, Jesus wasn't talking to just Saints Fans. He was trying to remind all of His disciples that life on Earth (not a football field) will be a constant struggle. Through faith and perseverance in times of hardship, true blessedness, true happiness in the Kingdom of God will be theirs. The Beatitudes is a list of warnings to all those who believe that this situational or temporal happiness is all that life offers. They will find themselves hungry and weeping when Christ comes again.

People of God, watching a football game can be fun even when you know that your favorite team doesn't really have a chance to win. But, ultimately, we all know that in the end, our enjoyment of football and the other forms of entertainment in this world will not matter.

Modern society does offer us a great deal of comforts and ways to be entertained. I firmly believe that most of our technological advances and exciting sports events are true gifts from God. Thus, it is appropriate for us to share in the joys of this world. What we must not do is to think that these joys and comforts are the only happiness that God and life has to offer. To do this would limit our hope to present times and diminish our true hope in the Resurrection.

On Super Bowl Sunday, thousands upon thousands gather around TV sets to watch and celebrate the physical and mental feats of football coaches and players. They spend three to four hours discussing football terminology such as Blocking and Extra Points, Two-Minute Warnings and Quarterback Sneaks.

Some begin watching TV in the morning and do not get up from their couches until later that night. That amounts to almost 10 hours of watching football and all of the hype that goes with it. Of course, these are the same folks who complain if Mass lasts longer than an hour.

If only they were willing to spend the same amount of time in Church, interpreting the terminology of Sacred Scripture and our Church's Teachings.

If only we could get thousands upon thousands to realize that as exciting as the Super Bowl may be, the Super Meal of the Eucharist is even more exciting.

For through this meal, you receive the necessary physical, mental and spiritual strength to play on the Battlefield rather than on a Football Field.

Today I pray, that you will realize that you are a First Round Draft Choice for God's Holy Team.

May the Saints of God coach you, and the Angels block for you.

May you avoid the illegal motions of sin and rejoice in the End Zone of Heaven.

And, if you need an extra point to win, I hope that you realize that one has already been scored for you. For, by hanging upon the Cross, Jesus secured Victory for our Team.

"Hey, People of God, your team has just won the ultimate Super Bowl. What are you going to do next?"

"I'm going to the Disneyworld of God.
        I'm going to Kingdom of Heaven!"

---

*Happy the man who finds wisdom,*

*the man who gains understanding!*
Proverbs 3:13

# Check Your Caller ID!

I want to address a growing problem in our community and in our Church, and that's the use of Cell Phones at inappropriate times. As a minister of God who has had the privilege of presiding at many great celebrations, I can tell you that as useful as cell phones can be, they are indeed becoming one of the greatest annoyances in many churches and in other public places.

In the movie theaters, ringing phones become a distraction. At music concerts, phones become distractions. And Lord knows that in church phones ringing can indeed break the moment of prayer and distract everyone from focusing on God and his people.

There have been times, especially at weddings and funerals, that I have had to really hold my tongue, when a phone begins to ring during the service. Often, I am with a loving couple who could be in the middle of saying, "I do," and "ring ring," a phone goes off and messes up that sacred moment. When you go to a funeral, you ought to be there focusing on the life of the deceased and praying for them to get into Heaven.

A ringing phone definitely takes away that focus. That is why before I start weddings, I often request that folks reach into their pockets or purses and either switch the ringer on their phone to vibrate or simply turn it off.

I even tell the old folks, "If you don't know how to work all of those things on your phone, turn to a young person next to you and let them do it for you." The last thing that we want is to have the service disrupted by a cell phone.

Also, if your phone is on vibrate, and someone does call you during Mass, it is not appropriate for you to actually answer the phone in Church. If it is an emergency, or a call that you just have to take, please excuse yourself from the pew and go outside and answer the call.

I have seen folks, young and old, who while sitting in Mass actually answer their phones and talk as if it is just a normal thing to do. Just because you think that nobody can see you as you lean down behind the back of the pews, it talk doesn't mean that we are not watching.

As my Momma would say, "Even if I don't see you, God does!"

To the young folks that think that it is cool to have "Hardcore Rap" songs as ring tones for friends and family, it ain't cool or even funny when your friend calls and the old lady next to you is subjected to a whole lot of cussing when both of you are supposed to be focusing on God.

And, while I am on the issue of cell phone usage, let me address text messaging in church. Texting someone during Mass is just as bad as talking to someone on the cell phone during Mass. Just because it is a quiet activity doesn't mean that it isn't distracting or appropriate to do in church.

*So, FYI, your BFF does not need to LOL*
  *when you are supposed to be talking to GOD!*[101]

And don't look at me with that IDK look on your face, you know what I'm talking about![102]

The use of cell phones in Church can and does become distracting. So, please be considerate of others whenever you come into a house of worship!

With that being said, I can now move on to my reflection. Because....LOL.....this reflection is actually about Answering the Call. No, not answering a cell phone call. *Answering the Call from God* to Know Him, Love Him and Service Him in this world so that we can all be happy with Him in the next!

But specifically, I want to talk about *answering the call to service Him* in Religious Life.

With all that is going on in the world around us, many people wonder whether or not God is still calling folks to Religious Life. Everybody is talking about the shortage of priests. Archdioceses are beginning to close churches and consolidate their manpower. Religious Communities of Sisters and Brothers seem to be shrinking every day.

The question is,
Has God somehow stopped calling folks to dedicate their lives to His service?

Just what is going on?

---

[101]FYI (for your information); BFF (Best Friend Forever);
LOL (laughing out loud); GOD (GOD)

[102]IDK (I don't know)

116

I assure you, God has not stopped calling. The problem is there is so much going on around us, *so many distractions*, that it is becoming harder and harder to hear His Voice through the loud pounding sounds of our modern technological world.

Maybe God should be using cell phones to call us to ministry. Maybe that would work better than His old methods of burning bushes or angelic visitors.

So, if your cell phone rings in Mass, and the Caller ID pops up with G O D . . . go ahead and answer that call or at least remember to *69 the Lord after Mass.[103]

A wonderful story about answering the call can be found in the Gospel according to our Brother Matthew. In Matthew 4:12-23, we hear the story of four men whose lives were consumed, not by modern technology, but by the technology of their day. They were consumed by the world and techniques of being professional fishermen!

Each came from a long line of fishermen and were probably following in their father's footsteps.

I would bet that they were pretty knowledgeable about the techniques of fishing and were able to provide olid incomes for their families by selling the fish they caught. The four men, that we hear about in Matthew 4:12-23, were Simon Peter and his brother Andrew, and James and his brother John.

All four grew up along the Sea of Galilee. Each day as young boys, they probably watched the fishermen pulling in their nets and hauling ashore the loads of tasty fish. They probably played along the sea casting off toy boats and fishing with their own little nets dreaming of the day when they would steer real boats and bring in loads of fish.

Well, that day did come. They did become fishermen. But with that day, came a *calling that changed their lives.*

One glorious day, as they worked with the nets in their boats, Jesus walked along the shore and began to call them to leave their boats and become His disciples. He said to them, *"Come after me and I will make you fishers of men."*[104]

---

[103]*69 refers to auto-dialing a return call.

[104]Matthew 4:19

He wasn't asking them to come to a special Sunday Service. He wasn't asking them to volunteer for the Temple's Fish Fry. He was asking them to abandon the dreams that once consumed their childhoods, cast aside the technology that they learned to use in their jobs and become His Apostles and aid Him in His ministry.

St. Matthew tells us that when they *got the call* from Jesus, they immediately abandoned their nets and became His followers.[105]

Imagine being at work or in school, sitting at your desk, and your cell phone rings. Looking at your phone, you see the name "Jesus" appear on the Caller ID Screen.

Knowing what we know today, it probably would be easy to answer that Call. But, for these first Apostles, it had to be a tough decision. They knew very little about this man from Nazareth. They had probably heard a few stories about His preaching and may have even seen John baptize Him. But, that was about it.

They did not have any of the modern technological things that we have to teach them about the Lord. It was tough for them to decide to give up steady jobs to follow a man, who in His own words, *had no place to lay His head.*[106]

There had to be something about Jesus that made them abandon their nets and follow Him. In a very real way, these four fishermen had to feel the presence of God. Although they didn't immediately realize that Jesus, the son of Mary and Joseph, the Carpenter, was actually the Son of God, they did feel God's presence in Him. And, it was this presence that they desired.

In Jesus, they felt the light that Isaiah proclaimed. In Jesus, they no longer walked in darkness.[107]

For, he was truly a Great Light: a Technically Spiritual Light which changed their hearts and gave them new dreams, and a light which shined on God's desires for them.

---

[105]Matthew 4:20

[106]In Luke 9:58, Jesus says, *"Foxes have dens and birds of the sky have nests, but the Son of Man has nowhere to rest His head."*

[107]See Isaiah 9:1

It would be a little while longer before Peter, Andrew, James and John would come to realize how great this Light of Christ was, and how far advanced His Technology would be! But, once they did realize it, they dedicated their lives to serving Him and eventually gave up their earthly lives defending Him.

My brothers and sisters, like those four fishermen, each of us is called by Jesus to become His follower. Each of us is called to be His disciples, to be those who use our gifts and talents (and even our technology) to spread the Good News.

But, are we willing to do as Peter, Andrew, James and John did and abandon our nets to immediately follow Him?

Are we willing to be His followers, regardless of the consequences that may happen?

Are we willing to give our entire lives over to Christ?

Unlike the four fishermen of old, Jesus is not asking you to leave your job and become itinerant preachers. But, what He is asking is that you be His follower regardless of what your job is.

This means that
> If you are a lawyer, be a lawyer for Christ.
> If you are a teacher, be a teacher for Christ.
> If you are a homemaker, be a homemaker for Christ.

Regardless of what your role in life is, regardless of what you do, do it in the name of Christ.

In every aspect of your life, technical or non-technical, you must be authentically Christian, authentically Catholic, and authentically true to the values and teachings that have been handed down to us from the days of the Apostles.

You cannot be an authentic Christian and still perform works which are against Christian beliefs. For, as Christians, we are known by our good works. Remember: *They will know we are Christians by our love.*

In my home parish of Our Lady Star of the Sea, God has called me, Deacon Melvin Jones and Deacon Brian Gabriel to serve Him at His Altar as ordained ministers. Our Calls did not come to us through a cell phone or some great technological thing. Our calls came to us through the ringing of the Holy Spirit in our hearts.

We were called to ministry when God chose to touch our hearts and awaken our desire to serve Him by serving you, His people. We were called to service at the Altar and I am positive that some of the people reading this book have a similar calling, a calling to the priesthood, the diaconate or religious life.

But, others are called to be of service to Christ and His Church in different ways. Some are called by God to be lay ministers in the Church by participating in the weekend Masses as Eucharistic Ministers, Readers, Choir Members, Ushers, Dancers and Altar Servers.

Others show that they are authentic followers of Christ by becoming members of Religious Education Programs, RCIA Teams, The Knights of Peter Claver and the Ladies Auxiliary, The Knights of Columbus and the Ladies Auxiliary, the Ladies Guilds, the Men's Clubs or Youth Groups.

There are many ways for us to follow Christ and to be of service to our brothers and sisters. It is up to each of us to not only hear the Call of Jesus, but to also answer it.

You know, it is hard to imagine how my life would be if I did not have a cell phone. In fact, on the rare occasions that I leave the rectory and forget my phone, I spend the entire time worrying that somebody might be calling me and I will miss the call because I don't have my phone.

I thank God that my Call to the priesthood was not dependant on having that cell phone or some other form of modern technology. Because, I may just have missed answering *THEEEE* Call because on the day that God decided to call me, I had forgotten my cell phone at home.

Plus, if I would have missed answering the Call to the priesthood, I would still be a public school teacher and Lord knows, I wouldn't be able to afford a fancy phone like the one I have!

Today, let us pray that God will help us move through the world of technology to hear and answer His Call to service. Let us pray that we will have the courage to answer that Call regardless of what we might have to leave behind in order to serve Him. And finally, let us pray that all who have *answered the Call* will have the strength and endurance to complete the Good Works that God has begun in them.

People of God, God is calling each of us to something special. It is time for you to pick-up your Spiritual Phones and Check Your Caller ID!

# My Funeral Plans

Back in April of 1995, just about a month before I was ordained to the priesthood, the Archdiocese sent me a bunch of forms to fill out for my upcoming new job.

There were forms for my health insurance, forms for my dental insurance, forms for my car insurance, forms on what personal property I owned, forms on what type of parish I wanted to be assigned to, forms on what I want to do for vacation, and forms on what I want to do in my future. I even think that there was a form on *how much I liked to fill out forms.*

When you are preparing to be ordained, the Archdiocese wants to gather as much information on you as they can, so that they can better place you in a parish where you can be successful as a minister.

As I filled out all the forms in the package, one of the forms really threw me for a loop. You see, in addition to all the forms that could help the archdiocese plan where they would assign me after I was ordained, there was also a form on which they wanted me to plan my funeral in case I suddenly died.

Talk about an eye opener.

As excited as I was about being ordained, all of a sudden I was being faced with planning my funeral. Wow!

You would think that they were already trying to get rid of me!

Well, as I stared at that form, I can remember thinking about what a funeral for me would entail. I thought about everything, from the music to the readings, and from the Homilist to the pall bearers. If there was going to be a funeral for me, I wanted it to be just right!

It was going to be a simple and quiet event because I'm such a simple and quiet man! OK, just go with the feelings!

Well, it's been a few years since I had to fill out that form. And, I guess that when I take time to update the funeral form, it will probably be a bigger plan than the funeral plan I had back in 1995. You see, that once humble and quiet seminarian has now blossomed into the one that can only be described as *"The Aura that is Tony!"*

Indeed, the plan that I have now for my funeral is a tad bit more extravagant than the one I had back in 1995.

When I go, I want a *throw-down* that is befitting of a Co-heir to the Kingdom. I want a party that folks will remember for decades. I want to go out in style!

First, I want a simple wooden coffin. A nice one can be ordered from the Benedictine Monks over at St. Joseph's Abbey in St. Benedict, Louisiana. Their coffins are beautifully modest. They are old fashioned and look really classy!

For the Funeral Mass, I would like a Jazz Band to play with the Gospel Choir. And, when the Church Celebration is done, I want a Second Line Parade with at least 20 women following the hearse crying profusely because such a good man is gone!

And, let us not forget my outfits. Yep, I said, outfits (with an "s").

Just like the late gospel musician, Raymond Myles had for his funeral, I want to wear at least three different outfits over the span of the three days that it will take to celebrate my Birthday into Heaven.

At the wake or vigil service, I want to be laid out in my Black Cassock, with the little cape flowing and a gold cross blazin'!

At the Morning Visitation, I want to be laid out in my Black Suit with my black Timberland Boots on my feet!

And for the Mass, I have to be laid out in Full Priestly Vestments with a wireless microphone on my head just in case I have something else to say!

When I go, I want folks to be talking for weeks about how good my funeral was and what a *throw-down* we had. Just like our Mardi Gras Masses, I want folks to walk out saying, *"Now, you know that boy just ain't right!"*

Oh, and I think that I am also going to preach my own funeral homily. By the time I go, I'll be able to leave behind a video or a hologram of me preaching from the pulpit.

Heaven forbid I leave it up to someone else to do me justice. Lord knows, can't nobody out preach the *Aura that is Tony*! Plus, can you see the Archbishop's face when he finds out that I am preaching at my own funeral!

People of God, each November, the Roman Catholic Church brings our Liturgical Season to a close. In the final weeks of our liturgical year, our Church calls all of us to reflect on what will happen to all of us at the end of time.

Will we truly be ready when the Savior decides to call us Home?

Are we prepared for the day that they will bury us?

Planning for your funeral is one thing. But, being prepared to die is truly another.

That is why St. Paul, in his First Letter to the Thessalonians, reminds us that we must be ready for our final days, because *"you yourselves know very well that the day of the Lord will come like a thief at night."*[108]

For most of us, we will not know that day nor the hour that the Lord will call us home.[109] We will not have time to plan for our funerals or even more importantly plan for our moment at the Judgment Seat. This means that we have to make sure that we are ready now, just in case today is our last day on Earth.

Like a *thief in the night*, the Angel of Death can creep up on us and usher us through the doorway that connects this world and the world of the Spirits.

Are you ready to stand before the Judgment Seat?
Are you ready to meet God, face to face?
Are you ready to account for what you have done in this world
as you supposedly were getting ready for the *world that is to come*?

Are you ready to answer questions like have you truly come to Know, Love and Serve Jesus as your personal Lord and Savior?
Simply put, are you ready to die?

In Chapter 25 of the Gospel according to our Brother Matthew stresses to us that for some, their moment at the Judgment Seat will usher in a harsh reality. In the Parable of the Talents, Jesus reminds us that everyone has been given certain gifts and opportunities by God.

What you do with all that God has given you will be a deciding factor in whether or not you make it into Heaven. That is why Jesus said to His Apostles,

---

[108]1 Thessalonians 5:2

[109]See Luke 12:46

*"Stay awake, for you know neither the day nor the hour. "It will be as when a man who was going on a journey called in his servants and entrusted his possessions to them. To one he gave five talents; to another, two; to a third, one--to each according to his ability. Then he went away. Immediately the one who received five talents went and traded with them, and made another five. Likewise, the one who received two made another two. But the man who received one went off and dug a hole in the ground and buried his master's money.*

*After a long time the master of those servants came back and settled accounts with them. The one who had received five talents came forward bringing the additional five. He said, 'Master, you gave me five talents. See, I have made five more.' His master said to him, 'Well done, my good and faithful servant. Since you were faithful in small matters, I will give you great responsibilities. Come, share your master's joy.'*

*(Then) the one who had received two talents also came forward and said, 'Master, you gave me two talents. See, I have made two more.' His master said to him, 'Well done, my good and faithful servant. Since you were faithful in small matters, I will give you great responsibilities. Come, share your master's joy.'*

*Then the one who had received the one talent came forward and said, 'Master, I knew you were a demanding person, harvesting where you did not plant and gathering where you did not scatter; so out of fear I went off and buried your talent in the ground. Here it is back.'*

*His master said to him in reply, 'You wicked, lazy servant! So you knew that I harvest where I did not plant and gather where I did not scatter? Should you not then have put my money in the bank so that I could have got it back with interest on my return? Now then! Take the talent from him and give it to the one with ten. For to everyone who has, more will be given and he will grow rich; but from the one who has not, even what he has will be taken away. And throw this useless servant into the darkness outside, where there will be wailing and grinding of teeth. "*[110]

---

[110]Matthew 25:14-30

Some have been blessed with monetary gifts.
How are you using your money for the sake of the Kingdom?

Some have been blessed with physical talents.
Are you using your gift of music, dance or creativity
for the sake of the Kingdom?

Some have been blessed with spiritual talents.
Are you using your gifts to bring others closer to God in prayer?

How are you using the blessing that God has poured down on you?

On the day that you die, will you be prepared to account for how well you used your gifts and talents?

Back in Jesus' day, the word "talents" literally referred to a some of money that was being used. I once read that a talent was equivalent to about fifteen years of wages for an ordinary worker. That's a lot for a Master to hand over to a worker and then just leave.

But, in the parable, Jesus was trying to stress how much trust the Master had in his workers. That's why although he returned unexpectantly, he still expected his workers to have done something productive with what he had given them.

As harsh as it may sound, the one worker who didn't do anything with what the Master had given him, really deserved to be treated they way he was treated. He deserved to be cast out of the Kingdom because he was too lazy to do what God needed him to do.

People of God, all of us are called to look at how God has blessed us in our lives and how we have chosen to use our blessings for the sake of the Kingdom. Because, my brothers and sisters, the day will come when you and I will have to stand before God and account for what we have done with the gifts that God has given us.

For some, it is a scary thing to think about the fact that one day we will die. But, the stark reality is that unless your name is Elijah, and you are expecting a *Fiery Chariot to swing low and carry you home*, you will die some day.[111]

---

[111]See 2 Kings 2:11

But, it is not the death part that you have to worry about. It's standing at the Judgment Seat with which you need to be concerned. So, today, I ask you, "Are you ready to die?"

Some folks think that I am joking about preaching at my own funeral. But, I really am not joking. Ya'll know that I am going to want to have to last word! But, more importantly, I want to make sure that when I die, folks really do remember what was important about my life.

You see, at my funeral, some will remember that I preached all across the nation and in about 20 other countries. Some will remember that I have preached before crowds as large as 20,000 teenagers. Some will remember that I wrote a couple of books and recorded sermons on tapes and CD's. Some will even remember that I was the pastor of not one but two of the greatest parishes in the Archdiocese of New Orleans.[112]

Indeed, they will remember a lot of what I have said and done partially because I am going to leave a list of stuff for them to read off at my funeral. But, for me, I am concerned that most will have never fully understood why I was able to do as much as I did. Some will never get as Kirk Franklin would put it, *"the reason why I sing."*[113]

And that's why I want to preach at my own funeral. Because, as great as it will be for folks to read off all of my accolades, awards and honors, the only thing that will matter in the end is if they knew just two things about me.

In fact, it's the two things that I want inscribed on my grave's headstone:
First: "He loved the Lord and the Lord loved him!"
And, second: "He was his *Momma's Baby*." After that, nothing really matters.

In the celebration of the Eucharist, Jesus continuously preaches to us about all that He wants us to know about Him. In this Blessed Feast, He tells us that He was, is, and will alway be the *"Lamb of God who takes away the Sins of the World."*[114]

---

[112]Our Lady Star of the Sea Church and St. Philip the Apostle Parishes in New Orleans.

[113]*"The Reason Why We Sing"* was a 1993 hit song for Kirk Franklin and The Family.

[114]John 1:29

That is why at His Last Supper, the last time that He got the chance to truly preach to His congregation of disciples before He died, He told them to *"Do this in Memory of Me."*[115]

If folks didn't remember anything about Him, He at least wanted them to remember that He was willing to sacrifice His life for the sake of the world. That is why, in the celebration of the Eucharist, we continuously preach the sermon that Jesus gave on the night before He died.

Today, I pray that God will help you to truly be prepared for the moment that you will stand before the Judgment Seat.

I pray that you will be able to account for all of the gifts and talents the Lord has given you and how you have chosen to use them for the sake of the Kingdom.

And, I pray that following His assessment of your gifts, the Lord will be able to look at you and say,

> *"Well done my good and faithful servant.*
> *Come and inherit the Kingdom that has been prepared for you*
> *since the foundation of the world."*[116]

You know, at my funeral, I really want a major party. I want folks to dress in bright colors and laugh and joke the whole time. From my three outfits to the women following the hearse, when I go out, I want folks to definitely remember that I was here!

But, even if all of that doesn't happen, I just want folks to remember that I did the best that I could do with the few little talents that God has given me.

Once the *Aura that is Tony* leaves this place, Lord knows that there will be a void here on Earth. But, can you imagine how excited the Angels will be when they realize that they'll be a new preacher in town?!

Watch out St. Paul, because a brother is on his way!
And, soon, there will be a pulpit in Heaven with my name on it!

May God help us all be ready for our final days! Amen!

---

[115]Luke 22:19

[116]See Matthew 25:19-34

# Fr. Tony: A Humble Servant of God

For those who do not know who I am, please let me take a moment to introduce myself to you.

I am the illustrious, Rev. R. Tony Ricard, M.Th, M.Div., (that's Master of Theology and Master of Divinity). I am one of the most notable priests of the Archdiocese of New Orleans and was ordained by Archbishop Francis Schulte in 1995.

I am the Pastor of Our Lady Star of the Sea Catholic Church located in the historic St. Roch Neighborhood in the City of New Orleans.

Here is some trivia for you. In 1999, I made history in the Archdiocese of New Olreans by being the quickest person to be appointed a pastor. No one had ever been appointed to lead a parish with only four years of ordination under his belt.

I was a New Orleans' public school teacher, and back in 1988, was named "Outstanding New Teacher" in the public school system.

I am blessed to be an extremely gifted Teacher, celebrated Preacher and phenomenal Revivalist.

I am nationally and internationally known!

So, as the young folks would say, *"You better recognize!"*

Did you know that I have preached in almost every part of the United States except for North Dakota and South Dakota? Hopefully, one day, I'll get there, too.

I've preached in Hawaii five times. God is Good!

Do you realize how hard it is to fly to the Islands of Paradise, be treated like a King, do my lil' thing and then before you get on a plane to come home, they give you a check and thank you for coming?

It is so hard to be me. But, I do it for the sake of the Kingdom.

I have also preached in and visited 20 other countries. In Canada, I am becoming the Billy Graham of the Catholic Schools System. They can't get enough of me. Man, I am good!

It's hard to believe that I have keynoted for more youth events than I can actually remember. I've preached to as many as 20,000 teenagers at one time. In November of 2007, I was blessed to be one of the keynote speakers for the National Catholic Youth Conference in Columbus, Ohio. Nothing on Earth can compare to holding the attention of an arena that was packed with 20,000 faith-filled teens. It is good to be me!

At the 2005 Los Angeles Religious Education Congress, I presided and preached for a Mass in the presence of Cardinal Roger Mahoney, Archbishop of Los Angeles. Also present were several of his brother bishops, a whole bunch of my brother priests and more than 10,000 adults from all across the nation. The day after hearing me speak in the main arena, one of the local Monsignors referred to me as the "Barack Obama of the L.A. Congress."

Ya'll must not know who I am!

I am now an internationally known preacher and noted author. I am the Founder and Director of Two Knights Publishing Company and KnightTime Ministries. Our two books, *MAXimum Faith: Prayers and Reflections by Young Katrina Survivors* and *I Still Believe: A Testimony of Faith After the Storm* are officially best sellers with more than 9,000 copies sold.

So, if you didn't already know it, "I'm a Big Dog."

I've led prayers in the presence of President George W. Bush, Governor Mike Foster, Mayors Marc Morial and C. Ray Nagin, judges, councilmen, and even a city-elected dog catcher.

I am the illustrious Rev. R. Tony Ricard,
*Priest Extraordinaire* and a big time *Momma's Boy!*

So, you better *sit-up* and recognize.

You better know who I am!
    And realize , just how blessed you are to be reading my book!

Oh, and by the way, I am also, the most humble person that you will ever meet.

That's me, Fr. Tony one of the Best Priests that you will ever come across, but also a very Humble Servant of the Lord.

You see, because I know the Lord and have spent time listening to His Love for me through Sacred Scripture, I have come to realize just who I am in His sight. And, that is a humbling experience. For, God made me in His image and likeness. I definitely have a purpose for being as great as I am!

In the Book of Sirach or as it is also called the Book of Ecclesiasticus, God says to each of us,

> "My child, conduct your affairs with humility,
> and you will be loved more than a giver of gifts.
>
> Humble yourself the more, the greater you are,
> and you will find favor with God. For great is the power of God;
> by the humble He is glorified."[117]

Such humility is a virtue that will help you overcome the giant obstacles a false sense of pride can put in your way. For true humility helps us realize that *"all of our help cometh from the Lord."*[118] But, don't get me wrong, the person who has real self-respect and recognizes his or her personal gifts, is indeed also a humble person.

True Humility is not shyly saying, "I am not worthy." And then, somehow, hiding all of your gifts under a bushel basket. No, true humility is to know the truth and then live in that truth.

A *truly humble person* is also different from a person who has a false level of pride. Being too proud of ourselves can block us from seeing the truth. But, not recognizing our gifts and blessings can also block us from seeing the truth.

The key is to know that True Humility and True Pride are actually the same thing!

In exhibiting the gift of genuine humility, we are able to better see our real gifts, the gifts of others and the many rewards we can receive through sharing our gifts and sharing in the gifted-ness of others.

---

[117]Sirach 3:17-19

[118]See Psalm 121:2

True Humility also allows us to listen more clearly to the Lord. A humble person is able to accept the Lord's commands as gifts which increase our worth in the eyes of others. God's commands also help us to be ready to receive the greatest gift, the gift of eternal life.

Thus, the truly humble person will align himself with the New Covenant and receive an invitation to the Heavenly Banquet that is referred to in the Gospel of Our Brother Luke.

> *On a Sabbath, Jesus went to dine at the home of one of the leading Pharisees, and the people there were observing Him carefully.*
>
> *He told a parable to those who had been invited, noticing how they were choosing the places of honor at the table.*
>
> *"When you are invited by someone to a wedding banquet, do not recline at table in the place of honor. A more distinguished guest than you may have been invited by him, and the host who invited both of you may approach you and say, 'Give your place to this man,' and then you would proceed with embarrassment to take the lowest place.*
>
> *Rather, when you are invited, go and take the lowest place so that when the host comes to you he may say, 'My friend, move up to a higher position.' Then you will enjoy the esteem of your companions at the table. For everyone who exalts himself will be humbled, but the one who humbles himself will be exalted."*
>
> *Then He said to the host who invited Him, "When you hold a lunch or a dinner, do not invite your friends or your brothers or your relatives or your wealthy neighbors, in case they may invite you back and you have repayment.*
>
> *Rather, when you hold a banquet, invite the poor, the crippled, the lame, the blind; blessed indeed will you be because of their inability to repay you. For you will be repaid at the resurrection of the righteous."*[119]

---

[119]Luke 14:1-14

Through the Covenant of Jesus Christ, St. Luke tells us that invitations have been sent out by God to those who will attend the Messianic Banquet with God the Father, God the Son and God the Holy Spirit.

Only those who are humble and in need of salvation will be there. Those who don't need Jesus will not be invited. Those who *think that they can make it on their own* will find themselves waiting outside of the Gates to the Kingdom.

No one should assume that they have already made it to the Heavenly Banquet. For making such an assumption can bring a level of false pride which will prevent us from knowing that only through Jesus can we be saved. The ones who will make it into the Heavenly Banquet will be those who realize that only through the Blood of the Cross are we made perfect and acceptable to God our Creator.

False pride has always been a block along the road to Heavenly perfection. People who truly believe that they are perfect are only deceiving themselves. Many of them use a sense of false pride as a means of self-defense or as a way of hiding a low self-esteem.

The prideful have to make themselves seem better than others because they actually feel that they are not as good as others. Truly humble people are the ones who are great. For, they know that God has blessed them in many ways. But, they also know that God has also blessed everyone else in one way or another. Thus, they don't have to pretend that they are better than the rest. They know that we are all great in the Eyes of God.

You know, I have come to realize that it is not really hard to be humble, (especially, when you are as good as I am).

For, truly Humble People, in the Eyes of God, are those who are able to recognize not only their gifts, but also their faults and failures and their total dependency on God. Thus, perfect humility, in the Eyes of God, brings salvation to us through the Gift of Christ which ultimately translates as perfection in the company of the Creator at the Heavenly Banquet Feast.

Wherever I go, I don't hesitate to tell folks that I am Good. I don't hesitate to tell folks that I am gifted. I don't hesitate to tell folks how lucky they are to be in my presence because of who I am.

Cuz', I really am Good.

"I am Good" because I really have worked hard to become the priest, the preacher and the teacher that I am. But, the real reason why I am "truly Good" is because I was made in the image and likeness of God.

I am a Child of God, a very gifted Child of God! And, no level of False Humility will ever make me stop telling folks just how blessed I am.

People of God, you too ought to feel free to tell folks just who you are.

Don't hide your blessings and gifts under a bushel basket.

You are blessed enough to have been invited to the Banquet Table here on Earth and in the Heavenly Kingdom. You are a very gifted Child of God.

That ain't false pride. That's the truth. And, you shouldn't have to hide it!

So, "if anybody asks you who your are," Tell them "I'm a Child of God!" And, through the Grace of God, you are headed to the Heavenly Banquet!

But, if they ask you who I am, first tell them "He's a Child of God!" and then let them know that I am the illustrious Rev. R. Tony Ricard, M.Th. M. Div., an extremely gifted Teacher, a celebrated Preacher and a phenomenal Revivalist.

And for that - *"They Better Recognize!"*

---

*When a man walks in integrity and justice,*

*happy are his children after him!*

Proverbs 20:7

# Fr. Tony's Pictures from High School

**St. Augustine HS**
*Marching 100*

**Class of 1982**

**St. Augustine's
Senior Prom
May of 1982**

**Junior Class
President
Homecoming 1980**

**A Freshman at
Tulane University**

**Fr. Tony playing the Vibraphone
Tulane University Concert Band 1983**

**Pepper Louise Ricard
A Very Unspoiled Rottweiler**

136

# I Still Believe!

## A Testimony of Faith After the Storm!

On August 29, 2005, life as I knew it was changed forever.

Never could I have imagined the pain and heartache that we, the **Katrina Survivors**, would have to endure.

Yet, somehow, we are surviving. Somehow, we are making it. And, somehow, **We Still Believe**!

We know that it is through God's Grace that we have been able to make it.

*As I look back on my post-Katrina journey, I realize now, more than ever, how much God loves us. The reflections in this book speak about keeping the faith in tough times.*

*As the old folks would say, "As long as there is a God in Heaven, I know that I am going to be alright!" With this faith, now offered to you is My Testimony of Faith After the Storm!*

### Rev. R. Tony Ricard, M.Th., M.Div.
A Priest of the Archdiocese of New Orleans *and* Hurricane Katrina Survivor!

# MAXimum Faith
*Prayers and Reflections by Young Katrina Survivors*

*edited with an introduction and prayers by*
**Rev. R. Tony Ricard, M.Th., M.Div.**
**and Mr. Chris A. Quest, II**

---

Proceeds from the distribution of the *MAXimum Faith* prayer book
and the book *I Still Believe!*
go towards providing academic scholarships,
assisting with youth ministry programs
and the continuation of the print/prayer ministries of
*Two Knights Publishing Co.*

For more information, please visit
www.FatherTony.com

# COMING 2010

## A Documentary Film by Cynthia Capen

A documentary film entitled **Father Tony** is currently in post-production in Los Angeles, California. It's an inspirational story of Father Tony Ricard, a black Creole New Orleans Catholic Priest, and Pastor of Our Lady Star of the Sea Catholic Church on St. Roch Street in the poor 8th Ward. For the past 4 years, independent producer Cynthia Capen and her camera crew followed and filmed the struggles and triumphs of Father Tony. The film is a collective and quite touching portrait of Father Tony's deep and abiding faith and his exuberate and often humorous style of preaching. His powerful gift for evangelical youth ministry is becoming nationally known.

In recent years, the image of the Catholic Priest has been blurred with scandals. This documentary film offers a fresh perspective on this millennial old vocation by delving into the life of a man who loves being a priest. Viewers will get an intimate glimpse of Father Tony's unshakeable faith during the most difficult test of his priesthood – the aftermath of Hurricane Katrina where he says he was transformed from a "boy" priest to a "man" priest. The documentary takes you on a journey of Father Tony's world including the culturally and historically rich City of New Orleans.

For further information contact:
Cynthia Capen – Executive Producer
Capen Communications
909.226.2941
cjc557@msn.com